BoD-Wissenschaftsbuch

BoD
Norderstedt

HARALD MAURER

DIE ARCHITEKTURTYPEN DES „SELF-ORGANIZING (FEATURE) MAP (SO(F)M)" NACH TEUVO KOHONEN

Autor:

Harald Maurer hat seinen Magisterabschluß an der Universität Tübingen im Jahr 2007 bei Prof. Dr. Dr. W. Hoering gemacht. Sein Studium umfasste die folgenden Fächer:
das Hauptfach Philosophie mit Schwerpunkt Wissenschaftstheorie,
das Nebenfach Informatik mit Schwerpunkt Neuro- und Bioinformatik,
das Nebenfach Jura mit Schwerpunkt Steuerrecht und
das Beifach vergleichende Religionswissenschaft mit Schwerpunkt Indologie.
Daneben hat er auch Studien betrieben in den Beifächern
Psychologie mit Schwerpunkt kognitive Neuropsychologie und Soziologie,
sowie in Mathematik und den Naturwissenschaften mit Schwerpunkt Biologie,
v.a. kognitive Neurobiologie.

Zur Zeit schreibt er als Doktorand im Fachbereich Philosophie und Wissenschaftstheorie an seiner Promotionsarbeit bei Prof. P. Schroeder-Heister und Prof. M. Bogdan mit dem vorläufigen Arbeitstitel:
„DIE KONSTRUKTIONSSKIZZE EINER INTEGRATIVEN THEORIE DER KOGNITION AUF DER BASIS DER THEORETISCHEN MODELLE IM KONNEKTIONISMUS UND IM SYMBOLISMUS UND DEN EXPERIMENTELLEN MODELLEN AUS DEN KOGNITIVEN NEUROWISSENSCHAFTEN".

Harald Maurer
Universität Tübingen
Wilhelm-Schickard-Institut für Informatik und Philosophisches Seminar
Abt. Logik und Sprachtheorie
Sand 13
72076 Tübingen
E-Mail: Harald.Maurer@informatik.uni-tuebingen.de

Impressum:

Bibliographische Information der Deutschen Nationalbibliothek

Die deutsche Nationalbibliothek verzeichnet diese Publikation in der Deutschen Nationalbibliographie; detaillierte bibliographische Daten sind im Internet über http://dnb.d-nb.de abrufbar.

ISBN 9783837021462
Herstellung und Verlag: Books on Demand GmbH, Norderstedt
www.bod.de

Vorwort

Das Buch stellt eine leicht überarbeitete Fassung meiner Studienarbeit dar, die ich im Fachbereich Technische Informatik bei Prof. Dr. M. Bogdan im Wintersemester 2003/04 und im Sommersemester 2004 an der Universität Tübingen geschrieben habe, bei dem ich mich ganz herzlich für die optimale Betreuung bedanken möchte. Es gibt erstmals einen umfassenden Überblick über die wichtigsten Architekturtypen der „Selbstorganisierenden (Merkmals-)Karte" (engl.„Self-Organizing (Feature) Map (SO(F)M))" des finnischen Ingenieurs Teuvo Kohonen, auch „Kohonen-Karte" genannt, die eine der bedeutendsten Modelle im Rahmen der Theorie der künstlichen Neuronalen Netzwerke darstellt. Es werden dabei die relevantesten Passagen aus den wichtigsten Artikeln der jeweiligen Autoren zitiert, die die zentralen Konzepte der diversen Architekturmodelle wiedergeben, und dann zusammengefaßt und kommentiert.
Eine aktuellere Version der Literaturangaben, bei der auch Architekturmodelle angeführt sind, die in den Jahren 2004-2008 hinzugekommen sind, wird in einem Manuskript (Architecture Types of T. Kohonen's Self-Organizing (Feature) Map SO(F)M") dargelegt, das auch einen kurzen Überblick über die Thematik bietet, einsehbar unter www-ls.informatik.uni-tuebingen.de/maurer.
Das Buch richtet sich vor allem an Fachwissenschaftler aus den Disziplinen (Neuro-)Informatik und kognitive Neurowissenschaften sowie an diejenigen, die sich für den Themenbereich der „Künstlichen Intelligenz" und der Robotik interessieren. Für Studenten bietet es darüberhinaus eine kurze Einführung in die Selbstorganisierende Kohonen-Karte.
Abschließend möchte ich mich noch bei meiner Mutter für das Korrekturlesen des Manuskripts ganz herzlich bedanken.

Tübingen, im Winter 2008/09   Harald Maurer

KAPITELVERZEICHNIS

Kapitelverzeichnis .... IV - VIII
Literaturverzeichnis .... IX-XXIX
Abkürzungsverzeichnis XXX

0. PROLOG UND MOTIVATION 1

1. BASALER ARCHITEKTURTYP: (BASIC) SELF-ORGANIZING (FEATURE) MAP
    (SO(F)M) NACH T. KOHONEN 2

2. ARCHITEKTURTYPVARIANTE I: GROWING SOM VARIANTS 6

 2.1 TYPVARIANTE I.I: GROWING ON A FIXED ((HYPER-)RECTANGULAR) GRID .. 6

  2.11 GROWING GRID (GG) NACH B. FRITZKE 6
  2.12 GROWING SELF-ORGANIZING MAP (GSOM) NACH H.-U. BAUER /
       Th. VILLMANN 7
  2.13 INCREMENTAL GRID GROWING (IGG) NACH R. MIIKKULAINEN /
       J. BLACKMORE UND (GROWING) LATERALLY INTERCONNECTED
       SYNERGETICALLY SELF-ORGANIZING MAPS ((G)LISSOM) NACH
       R. MIIKKULAINEN / J.A. BEDNAR / A. KELKAR / J. SIROSH ET. ALT. 8
  2.131 GROWING LEXICAL MAP (GLM) NACH I. FARKAS / P. LI 9
  2.14 GROWING (OR DYNAMIC) SELF-ORGANIZING MAP (GSOM) NACH
       D. ALAHAKOON / S.K. HALGAMUGE / B. SRINIVASAN / A.L. HSU /
       ET. ALT. 9
  2.15 GROWING (OR DYNAMIC) SELF-ORGANIZING MAP (GSOM)
       NACH A.L. HSU / S.K. HALGAMUGE 9
  2.16 GROWING SELF-ORGANIZING MAP NACH A. NÜRNBERGER ET. ALT. 10
  2.17 GROWING SELF-ORGANIZING MAP (GSOM) NACH J. MONNERJAHN 10
  2.18 STRUCTURE-ADAPTIVE SOM WITH DYNAMICAL NODE SPLITTING
       SCHEME NACH S.B. CHO 10
  2.191 GROWING MULTI-DIMENSIONAL SELF-ORGANIZING MAP UND
       QUASI-FOUR-DIMENSIONAL-NEURONCUBE (QFDN) NACH
       U. SEIFFERT / B. MICHAELIS ET. ALT. 10
  2.192 SPACE PARTITION NETWORK (SPAN) NACH Ts.-Ch. LEE /
       A.M. PETERSON 10
  2.193 INTERPOLATIVE ALGORITHM NACH J.S. RODRIGUES / L.B. ALMEIDA 11
  2.194 MORPHOGENETIC ALGORITHM NACH St. JOKUSCH 11

LITERATUR

1. L.D. ALAHAKOON / S.K. HALGAMUGE / B. SRINIVASAN: Unsupervised Self-Evolving Neural Networks. In: Proceedings of the Ninth Australian Conference on Neural Networks (ACNN'98), Brisbane, Austalia, February, 1998. 1998. PP. 188-96
[ALAHAKOON / HALGAMUGE / SRINIVASAN 1998.1]

2. L.D. ALAHAKOON / S.K. HALGAMUGE: Knowledge Discovery with Supervised and Unsupervised Self Evolving Neural Networks. In: Proceedings of the 5th International Conference on Soft Computing and Information-Intelligent Systems (IIZUKA'98). Vol. 2. World Scientific. Singapore. 1998. PP. 907-10
[ALAHAKOON / HALGAMUGE 1998.2]

3. L.D. ALAHAKOON / S.K. HALGAMUGE / B. SRINIVASAN: A Structure Adapting Feature Map for Optimal Cluster Representation. In: Proceedings of the International Conference on Neural Information Processing. 1998. PP. 809-12
[ALAHAKOON / HALGAMUGE / SRINIVASAN 1998.3]

4. L.D. ALAHAKOON / S.K. HALGAMUGE / B. SRINIVASAN: Dynamic Self-Organizing Maps with Controlled Growth for Knowledge Discovery. IEEE Transactions on Neural Networks. Vol. 11. No. 3. 2000. PP. 601-13
[ALAHAKOON / HALGAMUGE / SRINIVASAN 2000]

5. L.D. ALAHAKOON / S.K. HALGAMUGE / A.L.C. HSU / B. SRINIVASAN: Visualising Cluster Separation with Dynamic SOM Tree. 6th International Conference on Soft Computing (IIZUKA 2000), Iizuka, Fukuoka, Japan, October 1-4, 2000. PP. 257-63
[ALAHAKOON / HALGAMUGE / HSU / SRINIVASAN 2000.1]

6. L.D. ALAHAKOON / S.K. HALGAMUGE / A.L.C. HSU / B. SRINIVASAN: Automatic Clustering and Rule Extraction Using a Dynamic SOM Tree. Proceedings of the 6th International Conference on Automation, Robotics, Control and Vision (ICARCV 2000), Singapore, Nanyang Technological University. December 2000.
[ALAHAKOON / HALGAMUGE / HSU / SRINIVASAN 2000.2]

7. L.D. ALAHAKOON: Controlling the Spread of Dynamic Self-Organising Maps. Neural Computation & Applications. Vol. 13. No. 2. 2004. PP. 168-74 (mit einer Präsentation von H.F. LAM)
[ALAHAKOON 2004]

8. G. ANDREU / A. CRESPO / J.M. VALIENTE: Selecting the Toroidal Self-Organizing Feature Maps (TSOFM) Best Organized to Object Recognition. In: Proceedings of the IEEE International Conference on Neural Networks. Vol. 21. IEEE Computer Society Press. 1997. PP. 1341-46
[ANDREU / CRESPO / VALIENTE 1997]

9. G. De A. BARRETO / A.F.R. ARAÚJO: Time in Self-Organizing Maps: An Overview of Models. International Journal of Computer Research. Vol. 10. No. 2. 2001. PP. 139-79
[BARRETO / ARAÚJO 2001]

10. H.-U. BAUER / Th. VILLMANN: Growing a Hypercubical Output Space in a Self-Organizing Feature Map. Technical Report TR-95-030. International Computer Science Institute. Berkeley/CA. 1995 und in: IEEE Transactions on Neural Networks. Vol. 8. No. 2. 1997. PP. 218-26
[BAUER / VILLMANN 1995.1]

11. H.-U. BAUER / Th. VILLMANN: A Growth Algorithm for Hypercubical Output Spaces in Self-Organizing Feature Maps. In: F. FOGELMAN-SOULIÉ / P. GALLINARI (Eds.): Proceedings of the International Conference on Artificial Neural Networks (ICANN'95), Nanterre, France. Vol. I. 1995. PP. 69-74
[BAUER / VILLMANN 1995.2]

12. H.-U. BAUER / Th. VILLMANN: The GSOM-Algorithm for Growing Hypercubical Output Spaces in Self-Organizing Maps. In: Proceedings of the Workshop on Self-Organizing Maps (WSOM'97). Espoo, Finland, June 4-6. Helsinki University of Technology. Neural Networks Research Center. Espoo, Finland. 1997. PP. 286-91
[BAUER / VILLMANN 1997]

13. H.-U. BAUER / Th. VILLMANN: Applications of the Growing Self-Organizing Map. Neurocomputing. Vol. 21. 1998. PP. 91-100
[BAUER / VILLMANN 1998]

14. H.-U. BAUER / N. MAYER / M. HERRMANN / T. GEISEL: A Cortical Interpretation of ASSOMs. In: L. NIKLASSON / M. BODÉN / T. ZIEMKE (Eds.): Proceedings of the 8th International Conference on Artificial Neural Networks (ICANN'98). Skövde. Sweden. 2-4 September 1998. Springer. Berlin. 1998. PP. 961-66
[BAUER / MAYER / HERRMANN / GEISEL 1998]

15. H. BRAUN / J. FEULNER / R. MALAKA: Praktikum Neuronale Netze. Springer-Verl. Berlin u.a. 1996
[BRAUN / FEULNER / MALAKA 1996]

16. R. BRAUSE: Neuronale Netze. Eine Einführung in die Neuroinformatik. 2. Aufl. B.G. Teubner. 1995
[BRAUSE 1995]

17. J. BRUSKE / G. SOMMER: Dynamic Cell Structure Learns Perfectly Topology Preserving Map. Neural Computation. Vol. 7. No. 4. 1995. PP. 845-65
[BRUSKE / SOMMER 1995.1]

18. J. BRUSKE / G. SOMMER: Dynamic Cell Structures. In: G. TESAURO / D. TOURETZKY / T. LEEN (Eds.): Advances in Neural Information Processing Systems 7. MIT Press. Cambridge/MA. 1995. PP. 497-504
[BRUSKE / SOMMER 1995.2]

19. J. BRUSKE / G. SOMMER / I. AHRNS: On-line Learning with Dynamic Cell Structures. In: F. FOGELMAN-SOULIÉ / P. GALLINARI (Eds.): Proceedings of the International Conference on Artificial Neural Networks (ICANN'95). Vol. II. 1995. PP. 141-46
[BRUSKE / SOMMER / AHRNS 1995.3]

20. V. BURZEVSKI / Ch.K. MOHAN: Hierarchical Growing Cell Structures. In: Proceedings of the IEEE International Conference on Neural Networks (ICNN'96), Washington/DC, June 1996. IEEE Service Center. Piscataway/NJ. 1996.
[BURZEVSKI / MOHAN 1996]

21. O.A.S. CARPINTEIRO: A Connectionist Approach in Music Perception. CSRP 426. Ph.D. Thesis. School of Cognitive and Computing Sciences. University of Sussex. Falmer/UK. 1996.1
[CARPINTEIRO 1996.1]

22. O.A.S. CARPINTEIRO / H.G. BARROW: A Self-Organizing Map Model for Sequence Classification. COGS Technical Report. n.CSRP 424. 1996. PP. 1-14
[CARPINTEIRO / BARROW 1996.2]

23. O.A.S. CARPINTEIRO: A Hierarchical Self-Organizing Map Model for Pattern Re-cognition. In: L. CALOBA / J. BARRETO (Eds.): Proceedings of the Third Brazilian Congress on Artificial Neural Networks. UFSC. Florianópolis/SC, Brazil. 1997. PP. 484-88
[CARPINTEIRO 1997]

24. O.A.S. CARPINTEIRO: A Hierarchical Self-Organizing Map Model for Sequence Recognition. In: Pattern Analysis and Applications. Vol. 3. No. 3. 2000. PP. 279-87
[CARPINTEIRO 2000]

25. O.A.S. CARPINTEIRO / A.J.R. REIS / P.S.Q. FILHO: A Hierarchical Hybrid Neural Model in Short-Term Load Forecasting. In: Proceedings of the 8th Brazilian Sympo-sium on Artificial Neural Networks (SBRN'2004), September 29th – October 1st, São Luis. 2004.
[CARPINTEIRO / REIS / FILHO 2004]

26. H. CHEN / C. SCHUFFELS / R. ORWIG: Internet Categorization and Search: A Self-Organizing Approach. Journal of Visual Communication and Image Representa-tion. Vol. 7. No. 1. 1996. PP. 88-102
[CHEN / SCHUFFELS / ORWIG 1996]

27. H. CHEN / D.G. ROUSSINOV: A Scalable Self-Organizing Map Algorithm for Text-ual Classification: A Neural Network Approach to Thesaurus Generation. Cc-Ai, the journal for the Integrated Study of Artificial Intelligence, Cognitive Science and Applied Epistemology. Vol. 15. No. 1/2. 1998. PP. 81-111
[CHEN / ROUSSINOV 1998]

28. G. CHENG / A. ZELL: Multiple Growing Cell Structures. Neural Network World. Vol. 5. 1999. PP. 425-52
[CHENG / ZELL 1999]

29. G. CHENG / A. ZELL: Externally Growing Cell Structures for Pattern Classification. In: H. BOTHE / R. ROJAS (Eds.): Proceedings of the 2nd ICSC Symposia on Neural Computation (NC'2000), May 23-26, 2000, Berlin. ICSC Academic Press. 2000. PP. 233-39
[CHENG / ZELL 2000]

30. G. CHENG / A. ZELL: Externally Growing Cell Structures for Data Evaluation of Chemical Gas Sensors. Neural Computing & Applications. Vol. 10. No. 1. 2001. PP. 89-97
[CHENG / ZELL 2001]

31. S.-B. CHO: Self-Organizing Map with Dynamical Node Splitting: Application to Handwritten Digit Recognition. Neural Computation. Vol. 9. 1997. PP. 1345-55
[CHO 1997.1]

32. S.-B. CHO: Neural-Network Classifiers for Recognizing Totally Unconstrained Handwritten Numerals. IEEE Transactions on Neural Networks. Vol. 8. No. 1. 1997. PP. 43-53
[CHO 1997.2]

33. J.A.F. COSTA / M.L.A. NETTO / A.D.D. NETO / J.M. BARBALHO: Hierarchical SOM Applied to Image Compression. In: Proceedings of the International Joint Confe-rence on Neural Networks. Vol. 1. 2001. PP. 442-47
[COSTA / NETTO / NETO / BARBALHO 2001]

34. J.A.F. COSTA / M.L.A. NETTO: Clustering of Complex Shaped Data Sets via Kohonen Maps and Mathematical Morphology. In: B.V. DASARATHY (Ed.): Proceedings of SPIE: The International Society for Optical Engineering. Vol. 4384. 2001. PP. 16-27
[COSTA / NETTO 2001]

35. J.A.F. COSTA / M.L.A. NETTO / A.D.D. NETO: A New Structured Self-Organizing Map with Dynamic Growth Applied to Image Compression. In: Congresso Brasileiro de Redes Neurais, São Paulo, Junho de 2003, Aceito. 2003.
[COSTA / NETTO / NETO 2003]

36. W. DENG / W. WU: Document Categorization and Retrieval Using Semantic Microfeatures and Growing Cell Structures. In: Proceedings of the 12th International Workshop on Database and Expert Systems Applications (DEXA'01). Silver Spring /MD. IEEE Computer Society. 2001. PP. 270-74
[DENG / WU 2001]

37. D. DERSCH: Eigenschaften neuronaler Vektorquantisierer und ihre Anwendung in der Sprachverarbeitung. LMU München. Institut für Medizinische Optik. Diss. 1995
[DERSCH 1995]

38. J. DOPAZO / J.M. CARAZO: Phylogenetic Reconstruction Using an Unsupervised Growing Neural Network that adopts the Topology of a Phylogenetic Tree. Journal of Mol. Evol. Vol. 44. 1997. PP. 226-33
[DOPAZO / CARAZO 1997]

39. J. DOPAZO / H.-CH. WANG / J.M. CARAZO: Self-Organizing Tree Growing Network for Classifying Amino Acids. Bioinformatics. Vol. 14. No. 4. 1998. PP. 376-77
[DOPAZO / WANG / CARAZO 1998]

40. J. DOPAZO / H.-CH. WANG / L.G. De La FRAGA / Y.-P. ZHU / J.M. CARAZO: Self-Organizing Tree-growing Network for the Classification of Protein Sequences. Protein Science. Vol. 7. No. 10. 1998. PP. 2613-22
[DOPAZO / WANG / De La FRAGA / ZHU / CARAZO 1998]

41. J. DOPAZO / J. HERRERO / A. VALENCIA: A Hierarchical Unsupervised Growing Neural Network for Clustering Gene Expression Patterns. Bioinformatics. Vol. 17. No. 2. 2001. PP. 126-36
[DOPAZO / HERRERO / VALENCIA 2001]

42. I. FARKAS / P. LI: Modeling the Development of Lexicon with a Growing Self-Organizing Map. In: Proceedings of the Fifth International Conference on Computational Intelligence. 2002. PP. 553-56
[FARKAS / LI 2002]

43. R.T. FREEMAN / H. YIN: Adaptive Topological Tree Structure for Document Organisation and Visualisation. Neural Networks. Vol. 17. 2004. PP. 1255-71
[FREEMAN / YIN 2004]

44. B. FRITZKE: Let it Grow – Self-Organizing Feature Maps with Problem Dependent Cell Structure. In: T. KOHONEN / K. MÄKISARA / O. SIMULA / J. KANGAS (Eds.): Artificial Neural Networks. Vol. I. North-Holland. Amsterdam. 1991. PP. 403-408
[FRITZKE 1991.1]

45. B. FRITZKE: Unsupervised Clustering with Growing Cell Structures. In: Proceedings of the International Joint Conference on Neural Networks (IJCNN'91), Singapore, November 1991. Vol. 2. IEEE Service Center. Piscataway/NJ. 1991. PP. 531-36
[FRITZKE 1991.2]

46. B. FRITZKE: Growing Cell Structures – A Self-Organizing Network in *k* Dimensions. In: I. ALEKSANDER / J. TAYLOR (Eds.): Artificial Neural Networks. Vol. II. North-Holland. Amsterdam. 1992. PP. 1051-56
[FRITZKE 1992.1]

47. B. FRITZKE: Wachsende Zellstrukturen – ein selbstorganisierendes neuronales Netzwerkmodell. Dissertation. Technische Fakultät. Universität Erlangen-Nürnberg. Erlangen. 1992
[FRITZKE 1992.2]

48. B. FRITZKE: Wachsende selbstorganisierende Netzwerke. Arbeitsbericht des IMMD. Bd. 25. S. 9ff. Universität Erlangen-Nürnberg. 1992 (http://www2.informatik.uni-erlangen.de/ Research/Jahresbericht/1992/Selbstorganisierende Netze)
[FRITZKE 1992.3]

49. B. FRITZKE: Kohonen Feature Maps and Growing Cell Structures – A Performance Comparison. L. GILES / S. HANSON / J. COWAN (Eds.): Advances in Neural Information Processing Systems 5. Morgan Kaufmann. San Mateo/CA. 1993. PP. 123-30
[FRITZKE 1993.1]

50. B. FRITZKE: A Growing and Splitting Elastic Network for Vector Quantization. In: Neural Networks for Signal Processing. Vol. 3: Proceedings of the 1993 IEEE-SP Workshop (9/93), Maryland, Florida. IEEE Service Center. Piscataway/NJ. 1993. PP. 281-90
[FRITZKE 1993.2]

51. B. FRITZKE: Vector Quantization with a Growing and Splitting Elastic Net. In: Proceedings of the International Conference on Artificial Neural Networks (ICANN '93), Amsterdam, September 13-16, 1993.
[FRITZKE 1993.3]

52. B. FRITZKE: Growing Cell Structures – A Self-Organizing Network for Unsupervised and Supervised Learning. International Computer Science Institut. TR-93-026. Berkeley/CA. 1993 und in: Neural Networks. Vol. 7. No. 9. 1994. PP. 1441-60
[FRITZKE 1994]

53. B. FRITZKE: Growing Grid – A Self-Organizing Network with Constant Neighborhood Range and Adaptation Strenght. Neural Processing Letters. Vol. 2. No. 5. 1995. PP. 9-13
[FRITZKE 1995.1]

54. B. FRITZKE: A Growing Neural Gas Network Learns Topologies. In: G. TESAURO / D. TOURETZKY / T. LEEN (Eds.): Advances in Neural Information Processing Systems 7. MIT Press. Cambridge/MA. 1995.
[FRITZKE 1995.2]

55. B. FRITZKE: Growing Self-Organizing Networks – Why? In: M. VERLEYSEN (Ed.): European Symposium on Artificial Neural Networks (ESANN'96). D Facto Conference Services. Brussels. 1996. PP. 61-72
[FRITZKE 1996]

56. B. FRITZKE: Growing Self-Organizing Networks – History, Status Quo, and Perspectives. In: E. OJA / S. KASKI (Eds.): Kohonen-Maps. Elsevier. Amsterdam u.a. 1999. PP. 131-44
[FRITZKE 1999]

57. St. GROSSBERG: Adaptive Pattern Classification and Universal Recoding: I. Parallel Development and Coding of Neural Feature Detectors. Biological Cybernetics. Vol. 23. 1976. PP. 121-34 (auch in J.A. ANDERSON / E. ROSENFELD (Eds.): Neurocomputing: Foundations of Research. Kpt. 19. MIT Press. 1988. PP. 245-58)
[GROSSBERG 1976]

58. F.H. HAMKER: Life-Long Learning Cell Structures – Continuously Learning without Catastrophic Interference. Neural Networks. Vol. 14. No. 4/5. 2001. PP. 551-73
[HAMKER 2001]

59. S. HAYKIN: Neural Networks. A Comprehensive Foundation. 2nd Ed. Prentice-Hall, Inc. 1999
[HAYKIN 1999]

60. M. HERRMANN / R. DER / G. BALZUWEIT: Hierarchical Feature Maps and Non-Linear Component Analysis. In: Proceedings of the IEEE International Conference on Neural Networks (ICNN'96), Washington/DC, June 1996. Vol. 2. IEEE Service Center. Piscataway/NJ. 1996. PP. 1390-94
[HERRMANN / DER / BALZUWEIT 1996]

61. V.J. HODGE / J. AUSTIN: Hierarchical Growing Cell Structures: TreeGCS. In: IEEE Transactions on Knowledge and Data Engineering. Vol. 13. Iss. 2. IEEE Educational Activities Department. Piscataway/NJ. 2001. PP. 207-18
[HODGE / AUSTIN 2001]

62. V.J. HODGE / J. AUSTIN: Hierarchical Word Clustering – Automatic Thesaurus Generation. Neurocomputing. Vol. 48. No. 1-4. 2002. PP. 819-46
[HODGE / AUSTIN 2002]

63. A.L. HSU / S.K. HALGAMUGE: Dynamic SOM with Hexagonal Structure for Data Mining.
[HSU / HALGAMUGE 2001.1]

64. A.L. HSU / S.K. HALGAMUGE: Enhanced Topology Preservation of Dynamic Self-Organising Maps for Data Visualisation. In: Proceedings of the Joint 9th IFSA World Congress and the 20th NAFIPS International Conference. Vol. 3. IEEE, Piscataway/NJ. 2001. PP. 1786-91
[HSU / HALGAMUGE 2001.2]

65. A.L. HSU / S.K. HALGAMUGE: Enhancement of Topology Preservation and Hierarchical Dynamic Self-Organising Maps for Data Visualisation. In: International Journal of Approximate Reasoning. Vol. 32. No. 2-3. 2003. PP. 259-79
[HSU / HALGAMUGE 2003]

66. M.M. Van HULLE: Faithful Representations and Topographic Maps – From Distortion- to Information-Based Self-Organization. John Wiley. New York. 2000
[Van HULLE 2000]

67. H.-L. HUNG / W.-Ch. LIN: Dynamic Hierarchical Self-Organizing Neural Networks. In: The IEEE International Conference on Neural Networks (ICNN'94), Orlando, Florida, June 27-29, 1994. Vol. II. IEEE Service Center. Piscataway/NJ. 1994. PP. 627-31
[HUNG / LIN 1994]

68. M. ITO / Ts. MIYOSHI / H. MASUYAMA: The Characteristics of the Torus Self-Organizing Map. In: The 6th International Conference on Soft Computing (IIZUKA'2000). Iizuka, Fukuoka, Japan. October 1-4, 2000. 2000. PP. 239-44
[ITO / MIYOSHI / MASUYAMA 2000]

69. St. JOKUSCH: A Neural Network which Adapts its Structure to a Given Set of Patterns. In: R. ECKMILLER / G. HARTMANN / G. HAUSKE (Eds.): Parallel Processing in Neural Systems and Computers. Elsevier Science Publisher. Amsterdam u.a. 1990. PP. 169-72
[JOKUSCH 1990]

70. S. KASKI: Data Exploration Using Self-Organizing Maps. Dissertation. Helsinki Univ. of Technology. Department of Computer Science and Engineering. Laboratory of Computer and Information Science. Acta Polytechnica Scandinavica. Mathematics, Computing and Management in Engineering Series. No. 82. 1997
[KASKI 1997]

71. M. KELLY: Self-Organizing Map Training Using Dynamic k-d Trees. In: T. KOHONEN / K. MÄKISARA / O. SIMULA / J. KANGAS (Eds.): Artificial Neural Networks. Vol. II. North-Holland. Amsterdam. 1991. PP. 1041-44
[KELLY 1991]

72. Chr. KEMKE / A. WICHERT: Hierarchical Self-Organizing Feature Maps for Speech. Proceedings of the World Congress on Neural Networks (WCNN'93). Vol. 3. Lawrence Erlbaum. Hillsdale/NJ. 1993. PP. 45-47
[KEMKE / WICHERT 1993]

73. M.Y. KIANG / U.R. KULKARNI / M.K. GOUL / A. PHILIPPAKIS / R.T. CHI / E. TURBAN: Improving the Effectiveness of Self-Organizing Map Networks Using a Circular Kohonen Layer. In: R.H. SPRAGUE Jr. (Ed.): Proceedings of the 30th Annual Hawaii International Conference on Systems Sciences. Vol. 5. IEEE Computer Science Press. 1997. PP. 521-23
[KIANG / KULKARNI / GOUL / PHILIPPAKIS / CHI / TURBAN 1997]

74. M.Y. KIANG / U.R. KULKARNI / R.St. LOUIS: Circular/Wrap-Around Self-Organizing Map Networks: An Empirical Study in Clustering and Classification. Journal of the Operational Research Society. Vol. 52. 2001. PP. 93-101
[KIANG / KULKARNI / LOUIS 2001]

75. G.K. KNOPF / A. SANGOLE: Scientific Data Visualization Using Three-Dimensional Self-Organizing Feature Maps. In: IEEE Conference on Systems, Man, and Cybernetics. Vol. 2. Piscataway/NJ. 2001. PP. 759-64
[KNOPF / SANGOLE 2001]

76. T. KOHONEN: Associative Memory. A System-Theoretical Approach. Springer-Verl. 1977
[KOHONEN 1977]

77. T. KOHONEN: Automatic Formation of Topological Maps of Patterns in a Self-Organizing System. In: E. OJA / O. SIMULA (Eds.): Proceedings of the 2nd Scandinavian Conference on Image Analysis. Espoo: Suomen Hahmontunnistustutkimuksen Seura. 1981. PP. 214-20
[KOHONEN 1981]

78. T. KOHONEN: Self-Organized Formation of Topologically Correct Feature Maps. Biological Cybernetics. Vol. 43. 1982. PP. 59-69 (auch in: J.A. ANDERSON / E. ROSENFELD (Eds.): Neurocomputing: Foundations of Research. Kpt. 30. MIT Press. 1988. PP. 511-22)
[KOHONEN 1982.1]

79. T. KOHONEN: Analysis of a Simple Self-Organizing Process. Biological Cybernetics. Vol. 44. 1982. PP. 135-40
[KOHONEN 1982.2]

80. T. KOHONEN: Clustering, Taxonomy, and Topological Maps of Patterns. Proceedings of the 6th International Conference of Pattern Recognition, Munich. IEEE Computer Society Press.Siler Spring/MD. 1982. PP. 114-28
[KOHONEN 1982.3]

81. T. KOHONEN: Self-Organizing and Associative Memory. 1. Ed. Springer-Verl. Berlin u.a. 1984 (zit. 2. Ed. 1988)
[KOHONEN 1988]

82. T. KOHONEN / J.A. KANGAS / J.T. LAAKSONEN: Variants of Self-Organizing Maps. IEEE Transactions on Neural Networks. Vol. 1. No. 1. 1990. PP. 93-99
[KOHONEN / KANGAS / LAAKSONEN 1990]

83. T. KOHONEN / J.A. KANGAS / J.T. LAAKSONEN: SOM-PAK. The Self-Organizing Map Program Package. Version 1.0. SOM Programming Team of the Helsinki University of Technology. Laboratory of Computer and Information Science. Rakentajanaukio 2 C. SF-02150 Espoo. 1992
[KOHONEN / KANGAS / LAAKSONEN 1992]

84. T. KOHONEN: Physiological Interpretation of the Self-Organizing Map Algorithm. Neural Networks. Vol. 6. 1993. PP. 895-905
[KOHONEN 1993]

85. T. KOHONEN: Self-Organizing Maps. 1. Ed. Springer-Verl. Berlin u.a. 1995
[KOHONEN 1995.1]

86. T. KOHONEN: The Adaptive-Subspace SOM (ASSOM) and its Use for the Implementation of Invariant Feature Detection. In: F. FOGELMAN-SOULIÉ / P. GALLINARI (Eds.): Proceedings of the International Conference on Artificial Neural Networks (ICANN'95). Vol. I. 1995. PP. 3-10
[KOHONEN 1995.2]

87. T. KOHONEN: Emergence of Invariant-Feature Detectors in Self Organization. In: PALANISWAMI et. alt. (Eds.): Computational Intelligence. A Dynamic Systems Perspective. IEEE Press. New York. 1995. PP.17-31
[KOHONEN 1995.3]

88. T. KOHONEN: The Self-Organizing Map, a Possible Model of Brain Maps. Medical & Biological Engineering & Computing. Vol. 34. Suppl. 1. Pt. 1. 1996. PP. 5-8 und in: The 10th Nordic-Baltic Conference on Biomedical Engineering. June 9-13, 1996, Tampere, Finland.
[KOHONEN 1996.1]

89. T. KOHONEN: Emergence of Invariant-Feature Detectors in the Adaptive-Subspace Self-Organizing Map. Biological Cybernetics. Vol. 75. No. 4. 1996. PP. 281-91 und in: Proceedings of the IEEE Nordic Signal Processing Symposium (NORSIG '96). 1996. PP. 65-70
[KOHONEN 1996.2]

90. T. KOHONEN / S. KASKI / H. LAPPALAINEN: Self-Organized Formation of Various Invariant-Feature Filters in the Adaptive-Subspace SOM. Neural Computation. Vol. 9. 1997. PP. 1321-44
[KOHONEN / KASKI / LAPPALAINEN 1997]

91. T. KOHONEN / S. KASKI / H. LAPPALAINEN / J. SALOJÄRVI: The Adaptive-Subspace Self-Organizing Map (ASSOM). In: Proceedings of the Workshop on Self-Organizing Maps (WSOM'97). Espoo, Finland. June 4-6, 1997. Helsinki University of Technology. Neural Networks Research Center. Espoo, Finland. 1997. PP. 191-96
[KOHONEN / KASKI / LAPPALAINEN / SALOJÄRVI 1997]

92. T. KOHONEN: The Self-Organizing Map. In: E. OJA (Ed.): Neurocomputing. Special Volume on Self-Organizing Maps. Vol. 21. No. 1-3. 1998. PP. 1-6
[KOHONEN 1998]

93. T. KOHONEN: Self-Organizing Maps. 3. Ed. Springer-Verl. Berlin u.a. 2001
[KOHONEN 2001]

94. T. KOHONEN: Overture. In: U. SEIFFERT / L.C. JAIN (Eds.): Self-Organizing Neural Networks. Recent Advances and Applications. Physica-Verl. Heidelberg, New York. 2002. PP. 1-12
[KOHONEN 2002]

95. P. KOIKKALAINEN / E. OJA: Self-Organizing Hierarchical Feature Maps. In: Proceedings of the International Joint Conference on Neural Networks (IJCNN'90), San Diego, California, June 17-21, 1990. Vol. II. IEEE Service Center. Piscataway/ NJ. 1990. PP. 279-84
[KOIKKALAINEN / OJA 1990]

96. P. KOIKKALAINEN: Fast Organization of the Self-Organizing Map. In: A. BULSARI / B. SAXÉN (Eds.): Proceedings of the Symposium on Neural Networks in Finland. Finnish Artificial Intelligence Society, Helsinki, Finland, 1993. PP. 51-62
[KOIKKALAINEN 1993]

97. P. KOIKKALAINEN: Progress with the Tree-Structured Self-Organizing Map. In: A.G. COHN (Ed.): Proceedings of the11th European Conference on Artificial Intelligence (ECAI'94). John Wiley & Sons. New York. 1994. PP. 211-15
[KOIKKALAINEN 1994]

98. P. KOIKKALAINEN: Fast Deterministic Self-Organizing Map. In: F. FOGELMAN-SOULIÉ / P. GALLINARI (Eds.): Proceedings of the International Conference on Artificial Neural Networks (ICANN'95), EC2 & Cie, Paris, October 1995. Vol. II. 1995. PP. 63-68
[KOIKKALAINEN 1995]

99. P. KOIKKALAINEN: Tree Structured Self-Organizing Maps. In: E. OJA / S. KASKI (Eds.): Kohonen-Maps. Elsevier. Amsterdam u.a. 1999. PP. 121-30
[KOIKKALAINEN 1999]

100. Kl.P. KRATZER: Neuronale Netze. Grundlagen und Anwendungen. Carl Hanser Verl. München, Wien. 1990
[KRATZER 1990]

101. J. LAMPINEN / E. OJA: Fast Self-Organization by the Probing Algorithm. In: Proceedings of the International Joint Conference on Neural Networks (IJCNN'89), Washington D.C., June 18-22 1989. Vol. 2. 1989. PP. 503-507
[LAMPINEN / OJA 1989]

102. J. LAMPINEN: Feature Extractor Giving Distortion Invariant Hierarchical Feature Space. In: St.K. ROGERS (Ed.): Proceedings of the International Society for Optical Engineering (SPIE). Vol. 1469. Pt. 1. SPIE. Bellingham/WA. 1991. PP. 832-42
[LAMPINEN 1991.1]

103. J. LAMPINEN: Distortion Tolerant Pattern Recognition Using Invariant Transformations and Hierarchical SOFM Clustering. In: T. KOHONEN / K. MÄKISARA / O. SIMULA / J. KANGAS (Eds.): Artificial Neural Networks. Vol. II. North-Holland. Amsterdam. 1991. PP. 99-104
[LAMPINEN 1991.2]

104. J. LAMPINEN / E. OJA: Clustering Properties of Hierarchical Self-Organizing Maps. Journal of Mathematical Imaging and Vision. Vol. 2. No. 2-3. 1992. PP. 261-72
[LAMPINEN / OJA 1992]

105. J. LAMPINEN: On Clustering Properties of Hierarchical Self-Organizing Maps. In: I. ALEKSANDER / J. TAYLOR (Eds.): Artificial Neural Networks. Vol. II. North-Holland. Amsterdam. 1992. PP. 1219-22
[LAMPINEN 1992]

106. Ts.-Ch. LEE / A.M. PETERSON: Adaptive Vector Quantization Using a Self-Development Neural Network. IEEE Journal on Selected Areas in Communications. Vol. 8. 1990. PP. 1458-71
[LEE / PETERSON 1990]

107. Zh.-Q. LIU: Adaptive Subspace Self-Organizing Map and its Application in Face Recognition. International Journal of Image and Graphics. Vol. 2. No. 4. 2002. PP. 519-40
[LIU 2002]

108. St.P. LUTTRELL: Self-Organising Multilayer Topographic Mappings. Proceedings of the 2nd International Conference on Neural Networks (ICNN'88), San Diego. Vol. 1. IEEE Service Center. Piscataway/NJ. 1988. PP. 93-101
[LUTTRELL 1988]

109. St.P. LUTTRELL: Hierarchical Vector Quantization. IEE Proceedings-I. Vol. 136. No. 6. 1989. PP. 405-13
[LUTTRELL 1989.1]

110. St.P. LUTTRELL: Hierarchical Self-Organising Networks. In: First IEE International Conference on Artificial Neural Networks, 16-18 October 1989. British Neural Network Society, London. 1989. PP. 2-6
[LUTTRELL 1989.2]

111. St.P. LUTTRELL: Image Compression Using a Multilayer Neural Network. Pattern Recognition Letters. Vol. 10. 1989. PP. 1-7
[LUTTRELL 1989.3]

112. St.P. LUTTRELL: Derivation of a Class of Training Algorithms. IEEE Transactions on Neural Networks. Vol. 1. No. 2. 1990. PP. 229-32
[LUTTRELL 1990]

113. St.P. LUTTRELL: Self-Supervision Multilayer Adaptive Networks. DRA Technical Report 4467. (RSRE). Malvern/UK. 1991
[LUTTRELL 1991]

114. Chr. von der MALSBURG: Self-Organization of Orientation Sensitive Cells in the Striate Cortex. Kybernetik. Vol. 14. 1973. PP. 85-100
[von der MALSBURG 1973]

115. Chr. von der MALSBURG / D.J. WILLSHAW: How Patterned Neural Connections can be Set Up by Self-Organization. Proceedings of the Royal Society of London. Vol. B 194. 1976. PP. 431-45
[von der MALSBURG / WILLSHAW 1976]

116. Th.M. MARTINETZ / Kl.J. SCHULTEN / H. RITTER: Topology-Conserving Maps for Learning Visuomotor-Coordination. Neural Networks. Vol. 2. 1989. PP. 159-68
[MARTINETZ / SCHULTEN / RITTER 1989.1]

117. Th.M. MARTINETZ / Kl.J. SCHULTEN / H. RITTER: 3D-Neural Net for Learning Visuo-motor-Coordination of a Robot arm. In: Proceedings of the International Joint Conference on Neural Networks (IJCNN'89), Washington. Vol. 2. 1989. PP. 351-56
[MARTINETZ / SCHULTEN / RITTER 1989.2]

118. Th.M. MARTINETZ / Kl.J. SCHULTEN: Hierarchical Neural Net for Learning Control of a Robot's Arm and Gripper. In: Proceedings of the International Joint Conference on Neural Networks, Washington/DC. Vol. II. IEEE Service Center. Piscata-way/NJ. 1990. PP. 747-52
[MARTINETZ / SCHULTEN 1990]

119. Th.M. MARTINETZ / Kl.J. SCHULTEN: A „Neural Gas" Network Learns Topologies. In: T. KOHONEN / K. MÄKISARA / O. SIMULA / J. KANGAS (Eds.): Artificial Neural Networks. Vol. I. North-Holland. Amsterdam. 1991. PP. 397-402
[MARTINETZ / SCHULTEN 1991]

120. Th.M. MARTINETZ / Kl.J. SCHULTEN: Topology Representing Networks. Neural Networks. Vol. 7. No. 3. 1994. PP. 507-22
[MARTINETZ / SCHULTEN 1994]

121. St.J. McGLINCHEY / C. FYFE: An Angular Quantising Self Organising Map for Scale Invariant Classification. In: Proceedings of the Workshop on Self-Organizing Maps (WSOM'97), Espoo, Finland, June 4-6. 1997. Helsinki University of Technology. Neural Networks Research Center. Espoo, Finland. 1997. PP. 91-95
[McGLINCHEY / FYFE 1997]

122. St.J. McGLINCHEY: Transformation-Invariant Topology Preserving Maps. 2000
[McGLINCHEY 2000]

123. D. MERKL / M. KÖHLE: Visualizing Similarities in High Dimensional Input Spaces with a Growing and Splitting Neural Network. In: C. von der MALSBURG et. alt. (Eds.): Proceedings of the 6th International Conference on Artificial Neural Networks (ICANN'96). Bochum, July 16-19, 1996. Springer-Verl. Berlin u.a. 1996. PP. 581-86
[MERKL / KÖHLE 1996]

124. D. MERKL: Exploration of Text Collections with Hierarchical Feature Maps. In: 20th Annual International ACM SIGIR Conference on Research and Development in Information Retrieval (SIGIR'97). Philadelphia/PA, July 27-31, 1997. Vol. 7. 1997. PP. 186-95
[MERKL 1997]

125. D. MERKL: Text Classification with Self-Organizing Maps: Some Lessons Learned. Neurocomputing. Vol. 21. No. 1-3. 1998. PP. 61-77
[MERKL 1998]

126. D. MERKL / A. RAUBER: Uncovering the Hierarchical Structure of Text Archives by Using an Unsupervised Neural Network with Adaptive Architecture. In: Proceedings of the 4th Pacific-Asia Conference on Knowledge Discovery and Data Mining. Current Issues and New Applications. Springer-Verl. London. 2000. PP. 384-95
[MERKL / RAUBER 2000]

127. D. MERKL / M. DITTENBACH / A. RAUBER: The Growing Hierarchical Self-Organizing Map. In: S. AMARI et. alt. (Eds.): Proceedings of the International Joint Conference on Neural Networks (IJCNN'2000), Como, Italy, July 24-27, 2000. Vol. 6. IEEE Computer Society Press. Los Alamitos/CA. PP. 15-19
[MERKL / DITTENBACH / RAUBER 2000]

128. D. MERKL / M. DITTENBACH / A. RAUBER: Recent Advances with the Growing Hierarchical Self-Organizing Map. In: N. ALLINSON / H. YIN / L. ALLINSON / J. SLACK: Advances in Self-Organising Maps. Springer-Verl. 2001. PP. 140-45
[MERKL / DITTENBACH / RAUBER 2001.1]

129. D. MERKL / M. DITTENBACH / A. RAUBER: Business, Culture, Politics, and Sport – How to Find Your Way Through a Bulk of News? On Content-Based Hierarchical Structuring and Organization of Large Document Archives. In: Proceedings of the 12th International Conference on Database and Expert Systems Applications (DEXA'2001). Springer-Verl. Berlin u.a. 2001. PP. 200-10
[MERKL / DITTENBACH / RAUBER 2001.2]

130. D. MERKL / M. DITTENBACH / A. RAUBER: Uncovering Hierarchical Structure in Data Using the Growing Hierarchical Self-Organizing Map. Neurocomputing. Vol. 48. 2002. PP. 199-216
[MERKL / DITTENBACH / RAUBER 2002.1]

131. D. MERKL / M. DITTENBACH / A. RAUBER: Organizing and Exploring High-Dimensional Data with the Growing Hierarchical Self-Organizing Map. Proceedings of the 1st International Conference on Fuzzy Systems and Knowledge Discovery (FSKD'02). Singapore, November 18-22, 2002. 2002. PP. 626-30
[MERKL / DITTENBACH / RAUBER 2002.2]

132. D. MERKL / M. DITTENBACH / A. RAUBER: The Growing Hierarchical Self-Organizing Map: Exploratory Analysis of High-Dimensional Data. In: IEEE Transactions on Neural Networks. Vol. 13. No. 6. IEEE Press. 2002. PP. 1331-41
[MERKL / DITTENBACH / RAUBER 2002.3]

133. D. MERKL / M. DITTENBACH / A. RAUBER / Sh.H. HE: Adaptive Hierarchical Incremental Grid Growing: An Architecture for High-Dimensional Data Visualization. In: Proceedings of the 4th Workshop on Self-Organizing Maps (WSOM'2003), Hibikino, Kitakyushu, Japan, September 11-14. Springer-Verl. 2003. PP. 293-98
[MERKL / DITTENBACH / RAUBER / HE 2003]

134. R. MIIKKULAINEN: Script Recognition with Hierarchical Feature Maps. Connection Science. Vol. 2. 1990. PP. 83-101
[MIIKKULAINEN 1990]

135. R. MIIKKULAINEN: Trace Feature Map: A Model of Episodic Associative Memory. Biological Cybernetics. Vol. 66. 1992.
[MIIKKULAINEN 1992]

136. R. MIIKKULAINEN / J. SIROSH: Self-Organization with Lateral Connections. The University of Texas at Austin, Austin/TX. Technical Report AI92 – 191. 1992
[MIIKKULAINEN / SIROSH 1992]
137. R. MIIKKULAINEN: Subsymbolic Natural Language Processing: An Integrated Model of Scripts, Lexicon, and Memory. MIT-Press. Cambridge/MA. 1993
[MIIKKULAINEN 1993]
138. R. MIIKKULAINEN / J. SIROSH: How Lateral Interactions Develops in a Self-Organizing Feature Map. In: Proceedings of the IEEE International Conference on Neural Networks (ICNN'93). Vol. III. IEEE Service Center. Piscataway/NJ. 1993. PP. 1360-65
[MIIKKULAINEN / SIROSH 1993]
139. R. MIIKKULAINEN / J. BLACKMORE: Incremental Grid Growing: Encoding High-Dimensional Structure into a Two-Dimensional Feature Map. TR AI92-192. University of Texas. Austin/TX. 1992 und in: Proceedings of the IEEE International Conference on Neural Networks (ICNN'93). Vol. I. IEEE Service Center. Piscataway/NJ. 1993. PP. 450-55
[MIIKKULAINEN / BLACKMORE 1993]
140. R. MIIKKULAINEN / J. SIROSH: Self-Organizing Feature Maps with Lateral Connections: Modeling Ocular Dominance. In: M.C. MOZER / P. SMOLENSKY et. alt. (Eds.): Proceedings of the Connectionist Models Summer School, Boulder, Colorado, June 1993. Lawrence Erlbaum. Hillsdale/NJ. 1994. PP. 31-38
[MIIKKULAINEN / SIROSH 1994]
141. R. MIIKKULAINEN / J. BLACKMORE: Visualizing High-Dimensional Structure with the Incremental Grid Growing Neural Network. In: A. PRIEDITIS / S. RUSSELL: Machine Learning. Proceedings of the Twelfth International Conference on Machine Learning. Morgan Kaufmann. San Francisco/CA. 1995. PP. 55-63
[MIIKKULAINEN / BLACKMORE 1995]
142. R. MIIKKULAINEN / Y. CHOE / J. SIROSH: Laterally Interconnected Self-Organizing Maps in Hand-Written Digit Recognition. In: D.S. TOURETZKY / M.C. MOZER / M.E. HASSELMO (Eds.): Advances in Neural Information Processing Systems 8 (NIPS'95). Proceedings of the 1995 Conference. MIT Press. Cambridge/MA. 1996. PP. 736-42
[MIIKKULAINEN / CHOE / SIROSH 1996]
143. R. MIIKKULAINEN / J.A. BEDNAR / A. KELKAR: Modeling Large Cortical Networks with Growing Self-Organizing Maps. Neurocomputing. Vol. 44-46. 2002. PP. 315-21
[MIIKKULAINEN / BEDNAR / KELKAR 2002]
144. R. MIIKKULAINEN / J.A. BEDNAR / A. KELKAR: Scaling Self-Organizing Maps to Model Large Cortical Networks. Neuroinformatics. Vol. 2. No. 3. 2004. PP. 275-302
[MIIKKULAINEN / BEDNAR / KELKAR 2004]
145. T. MIKAMI / M. WADA: Data Visualization Method for Growing Self-Organizing Networks with Ant Clustering Algorithm. In: J. KELEMEN / P. SOSIK (Eds.): Advances in Artificial Life. Proceedings of the 6th European Conference (ECAL' 2001), Prague, September 10-14, 2001. Springer-Verl. Berlin u.a. 2001. PP. 623-26
[MIKAMI / WADA 2001]

146. J. MONNERJAHN: Rectangular Self-Organizing Maps with a Flexible Network Size. In: B. KRIEG-BRÜCKNER / G. ROTH / H. SCHWEGLER (Hrsg.): ZKW Bericht Nr. 4/96. Universität Bremen. Zentrum für Kognitionswissenschaften (ZKW). 1996
[MONNERJAHN 1996]

147. B. MÜLLER / J. REINHARDT / M.T. STRICKLAND: Neural Networks. An Introduction. Springer-Verlag. Berlin, Heidelberg. 1995
[MÜLLER / REINHARDT / STRICKLAND 1995]

148. V.-E. NEAGOE: A Circular Kohonen Network for Image Vector Quantization. In: E. D'HOLLANDER et. alt. (Eds.): Parallel Computing: State-of-the-Art and Perspectives. Elsevier. Amsterdam u.a. 1996. PP. 677-80
[NEAGOE 1996]

149. A. NÜRNBERGER: Interactive Text Retrieval Supported by Growing Self-Organizing Maps. In: T. OJALA (Ed.): Proceedings of the International Workshop on Information Retrieval (IR'2001). Infotech. Oulu, Finland. 2001. PP. 61-70
[NÜRNBERGER 2001]

150. A. NÜRNBERGER / M. DETYNIECKI: Visualizing Changes in Data Collections Using Growing Self-Organizing Maps. In: Proceedings of the International Joint Conference on Neural Networks (IJCNN'02). Vol. 2. 2002. PP. 1912-17
[NÜRNBERGER / DETYNIECKI 2002]

151. E. OJA (Ed.): Neurocomputing. Special Volume on Self-Organizing Maps. Vol. 21. Nos, 1-3 October 1998. 1998
[OJA 1998]

152. E. OJA / S. KASKI (Eds.): Kohonen-Maps. Elsevier. Amsterdam u.a. 1999
[OJA / KASKI 1999.1]

153. E. OJA / J. LAAKSONEN / M. KOSKELA: Application of Tree Structured Self-Organizing Maps in Content-Based Image Retrieval. In: Proceedings of the Ninth International Conference on Artificial Neural Networks (ICANN'99). Vol. 1. Edinburgh/UK, September , 7-10, 1999. 1999. PP. 174-79
[OJA / LAAKSONEN / KOSKELA 1999.2]

154. E. OJA / J. LAAKSONEN / M. KOSKELA: Content-Based Image Retrieval Using Self-Organizing Maps. In: Proceedings of the Third International Conference on Visual Information Systems (VISUAL'99). Amsterdam, June 1999. 1999.
[OJA / LAAKSONEN / KOSKELA 1999.3]

155. E. OJA / J. LAAKSONEN / M. KOSKELA: PicSOM: Self-Organizing Maps for Content-Based Image Retrieval. In: Proceedings of the International Joint Conference on Neural Networks (IJCNN'99), Washington/ DC, July 1999. 1999.
[OJA / LAAKSONEN / KOSKELA 1999.4]

156. E. OJA / J. LAAKSONEN / M. KOSKELA: PicSOM – A Framework for Content-Based Image Database Retrieval Using Self-Organizing Maps. In: Proceedings of the 11th Scandinavian Conference on Image Analysis (SCIA'99), Kangerlussuaq, Greenland, June 1999. 1999.
[OJA / LAAKSONEN / KOSKELA 1999.5]

157. E. OJA / M. KOSKELA / J. LAAKSONEN / S. LAAKSO: The PicSOM Retrieval System: Description and Evaluations. In: J.P. EAKINS / P.G.B. ENSER (Eds.):Proceedings of Challenge of Image Retrieval (CIR 2000). Brighton/UK, May 2000. 2000.
[OJA / KOSKELA / LAAKSONEN / LAAKSO 2000]

158. J. ONTRUP / H. RITTER: Text Categorization and Semantic Browsing with Self-Organizing Maps on Non-Euclidean Spaces. In: L. De RAEDT / A. SIEBES (Eds.): Proceedings of the Fifth European Conference on Principles of Data Mining and Knowledge Discovery (PKDD'01). Springer-Verl. Berlin u.a. 2001. PP. 338-49
[ONTRUP / RITTER 2001.1]

159. J. ONTRUP / H. RITTER: Hyperbolic Self-Organizing Maps for Semantic Navigation. Advances in Neural Information Processing Systems. Vol. 14. 2001.
[ONTRUP / RITTER 2001.2]

160. J. ONTRUP / H. RITTER: A Hierarchically Growing Hyperbolic Self-Organizing Map for Rapid Structuring of Large Data Sets. In: Proceedings of the 5th Workshop on Self-Organizing Maps (WSOM'05). September 2005 .
[ONTRUP / RITTER 2005]

161. J. PAKKANEN: The Evolving Tree: A New Kind of Self-Organizing Neural Network. In: Proceedings of the Workshop on Self-Organizing Maps. Kitakyushu, Japan, September 2003. 2003. PP. 311-16
[PAKKANEN 2003]

162. J. PAKKANEN / E. OJA / J. IIVARINEN: The Evolving Tree – A Novel Self-Organizing Network for Data Analysis. Neural Processing Letters. Vol. 20. No. 3. 2004. PP. 199-211
[PAKKANEN / OJA / IIVARINEN 2004]

163. E. PAMPALK / G. WIDMER / A. CHAN: A New Approach to Hierarchical Clustering and Structuring of Data with Self-Organizing Maps. Intelligent Data Analysis. Vol. 8. No. 2. 2004. PP. 131-49
[PAMPALK / WIDMER / CHAN 2004]

164. J. RAHMEL: SplitNET: A Dynamic Hierarchical Network Model. In: Proceedings of the Thirteen National Conference on Artificial Intelligence and the Eight Innovative Applications of Artificial Intelligence Conference (AAAI'96). Vol. 2. AAAI Press / The MIT Press. Menlo Park u.a. 1996. P. 1404
[RAHMEL 1996.1]

165. J. RAHMEL: SplitNET: Learning of Tree Structured Kohonen Chains. In: IEEE International Conference on Neural Networks, Washington/DC, June 3-6, 1996. 1996. PP. 1221-26
[RAHMEL 1996.2]

166. H. RITTER / Th. MARTINETZ / Kl. SCHULTEN: Neuronale Netze. Eine Einführung in die Neuroinformatik selbstorganisierender Netzwerke. Addison-Wesley Publishing Company. Bonn u.a. 1990 (engl.: Neural Computation and Self-Organizing Maps: An Introduction. Addison-Wesley. Reading/MA. 1992)
[RITTER / MARTINETZ / SCHULTEN 1990]

167. H. RITTER: Learning with the Self-Organizing Map. In: T. KOHONEN / K. MÄKISARA / O. SIMULA / J. KANGAS (Eds.): Artificial Neural Networks. North-Holland. Amsterdam. 1991. PP. 379-84
[RITTER 1991]

168. H. RITTER: Parametrized Self-Organizing Maps. In: S. GIELEN / B. KAPPEN (Eds.): Proceedings of the International Conference on Artificial Neural Networks (ICANN'93). Amsterdam, 13-16 September 1993. Springer-Verl. London/UK u.a. 1993. PP. 568-77
[RITTER 1993]

169. H. RITTER / J. WALTER: Local PSOMs and Chebyshev PSOMs – Improving the Parametrised Self-Organizing Maps. In: F. FOGELMAN-SOULIÉ / P. GALLINARI (Eds.): Proceedings of the International Conference on Artificial Neural Networks (ICANN'95), EC2 & Cie, Paris, October 1995. Vol. 1. 1995. PP. 95-102
[RITTER / WALTER 1995]

170. H. RITTER / J. WALTER: Rapid Learning with Parametrized Self-Organizing Maps. Neurocomputing. Vol. 12. 1996. PP. 131-53
[RITTER / WALTER 1996.1]

171. H. RITTER / J. WALTER: Investment Learning with Hierarchical PSOM. In: D.S. TOU-RETZKY / M.C. MOZER / M.E. HASSELMO (Eds.): Advances in Neural Information Processing Systems 8 (NIPS'95). Proceedings of the 1995 Conference. MIT Press. Cambridge/MA. 1996. PP. 570-76
[RITTER / WALTER 1996.2]

172. H. RITTER / J. WALTER: Associative Completion and Investment Learning Using PSOMs. In: Proceedings of the International Conference on Artificial Neural Networks (ICANN'96). 1996. PP. 157-64
[RITTER / WALTER 1996.3]

173. H. RITTER: Self-Organizing Maps for Robot Control. In: W. GERSTNER et. alt. (Eds.): Proceedings of the 7th International Conference on Artificial Neural Networks (ICANN'97). Lausanne, Switzerland, October 8-10, 1997. Springer-Verl. 1997. PP. 675-84
[RITTER 1997]

174. H. RITTER: Self-Organizing Maps on Non-Euclidean Spaces. In: E. OJA / S. KASKI (Eds.): Kohonen-Maps. Elsevier. Amsterdam u.a. 1999. PP. 97-110
[RITTER 1999]

175. H. RITTER / J. WALTER / CI. NÖLKER: The PSOM Algorithm and Applications. Proceedings of the Symposium on Neural Computation. 2000. PP. 758-64
[RITTER / WALTER / NÖLKER 2000]

176. J.S. RODRIGUES / L.B. ALMEIDA: Improving the Learning Speed in Topological Maps of Patterns. In: Proceedings of the International Neural Networks Conference (INNC'90), Paris. Kluwer. Dordrecht, Boston. 1990. PP. 813-16
[RODRIGUES / ALMEIDA 1990]

177. R. ROJAS: Theorie der neuronalen Netze. Eine systematische Einführung. Springer-Verlag. Berlin u.a. 1993
[ROJAS 1993]

178. T. SAITO / R. OHTA: A Growing Self-Organizing Algorithm for Dynamic Clustering. In: Proceedings of the International Joint Conference on Neural Networks (IJCNN'2001). Vol. 1. 2001. PP. 469-73
[SAITO / OHTA 2001]

179. A. SCHERER: Neuronale Netze. Grundlagen und Anwendungen. Vieweg. Braunschweig, Wiesbaden. 1997
[SCHERER 1997]

180. U. SEIFFERT / B. MICHAELIS: Three-Dimensional Self-Organizing Maps for Classification of Image Properties. In: N.K. KASABOV / G. COGHILL (Eds.): Proceedings of the Second New Zealand International Two-Stream Conferene on Artificial Neural Networks and Expert Systems. IEEE Computer Society Press. Los Alamitos/ CA. 1995. PP. 310-13
[SEIFFERT / MICHAELIS 1995]

181. U. SEIFFERT / B. MICHAELIS: Growing 3D-SOM's with 2D-Input Layer as a Classification Tool in a Motion Detection System. In: A.B. BULSARI (Ed.): Proceedings of the International Conference on Engineering Applications of Neural Networks (EANN'96). Abo Akademis Tryckeri. Turku, Finland. 1996. PP. 351-54
[SEIFFERT / MICHAELIS 1996]

182. U. SEIFFERT / B. MICHAELIS / St. SCHÜNEMANN: Two More Modifications of SOM's to Handle Signals with Special Properties. Proceedings of the Workshop on Self-Organizing Maps (WSOM'97), Espoo, Finland, June 4-6, 1997. HUT, Helsinki. 1997. PP. 292-97
[SEIFFERT / MICHAELIS / SCHÜNEMANN 1997]

183. U. SEIFFERT / B. MICHAELIS: Quasi-Four-Dimensional- Neuroncube and its Application to Motion Estimation. In: Proceedings of the International Conference on Engineering Applications of Neural Networks (EANN'98). Systems Engineering Association. Turku, Finland. 1998. PP. 78-81
[SEIFFERT / MICHAELIS 1998.1]

184. U. SEIFFERT / B. MICHAELIS: Growing Multi-Dimensional Self-Organizing Maps. International Journal of Knowledge-Based Intelligent Engineering Systems. Vol. 2. No. 1. 1998. PP. 42-48
[SEIFFERT / MICHAELIS 1998.2]

185. U. SEIFFERT: Wachsende mehrdimensionale Selbstorganisierende Karten zur Analyse bewegter Szenen. In: http://iesk.et.uni-magdeburg.de/~seiffert/diss98. Html
[SEIFFERT 1998]

186. U. SEIFFERT: Growing Multi-Dimensional Self-Organizing Maps for Motion Detection. In: U. SEIFFERT / L.C. JAIN (Eds.): Self-Organizing Neural Networks. Recent Advances and Applications. Physica-Verl. Heidelberg, New York. 2002. PP. 95-120
[SEIFFERT 2002]

187. J. SI / S. LIN / M.-A. VUONG: Dynamic Topology Representing Networks. Neural Networks. Vol. 13. No. 6. 2000. PP. 617-27
[SI / LIN / VUONG 2000]

188. H.-H. SONG / S.-Wh. LEE: A Self-Organizing Neural Tree for Large Set Pattern Classification. IEEE Transactions on Neural Networks. Vol. 9. No. 3. 1998. PP. 369-80
[SONG / LEE 1998]

189. H. SPECKMANN / G. RADDATZ / W. ROSENSTIEL: Improvement of Learning Results of the Selforganizing Map by Calculating Fractal Dimensions. In: M. VERLEYSEN (Ed.): European Symposium on Artificial Neural Networks (ESANN'94). Conference Services. Brussells, Belgium. 1994. PP. 251-55
[SPECKMANN / RADDATZ / ROSENSTIEL 1994.1]

190. H. SPECKMANN / G. RADDATZ / W. ROSENSTIEL: Considerations of Geometrical and Fractal Dimension of SOM to Get Better Learning Results. In: M. MARINARO / P.G. MORASSO (Eds.): Proceedings of the International Conference on Artificial Neural Networks (ICANN'94), Sorrento, Italy, 26-29 May 1994. Vol. I. Springer-Verl. London u.a. 1994. PP. 342-45
[SPECKMANN / RADDATZ / ROSENSTIEL 1994.2]

191. H. SPECKMANN / G. RADDATZ / W. ROSENSTIEL: Relations between Generalized Fractal Dimensions and Kohonen's Self-Organizing Map. Neural Networks and their Applications, Marseilles, 15-16 December 1994. 1994. PP.151-60
[SPECKMANN / RADDATZ / ROSENSTIEL 1994.3]

192. H. SPECKMANN: Analyse mit fraktalen Dimensionen und Parallelisierung von Kohonens selbstorganisierender Karte. Dissertation. 1995
[SPECKMANN 1995]

193. H. SPECKMANN: Dem Denken abgeschaut. Neuronale Netze im praktischen Einsatz. Vieweg-Verl. Braunschweig, Wiesbaden. 1996
[SPECKMANN 1996]

194. M.-Ch. SU / H.-T. CHANG: A New Model of Self-Organizing Neural Network and its Application in Data Projection. IEEE Transactions on Neural Networks. Vol. 12. No. 1. 2001. PP. 153-58
[SU / CHANG 2001]

195. P.N. SUGANTHAN: Hierarchical Self Organising Maps. In: Proceedings of the Ninth Australian Conference on Neural Networks (ACNN'98). Univ. Queensland, Brisbane/QLD. 1998. PP. 255-59
[SUGANTHAN 1998]

196. P.N. SUGANTHAN: Hierarchical Overlapped SOM's for Pattern Classification. IEEE Transactions on Neural Networks. Vol. 10. No. 1. 1999. PP. 193-96
[SUGANTHAN 1999]

197. M. TAKATSUKA / R.A. JARVIS: Hierarchical Neural Networks for Learning three-dimensional Objects from Range Images. Journal of Electronic Imaging. Vol. 7. No.1. 1998. PP. 16-28
[TAKATSUKA / JARVIS 1998]

198. M. TAKATSUKA / R.A. JARVIS: Encoding 3D Structural Information Using Multiple Self-Organizing Feature Maps. Image and Vision Computing. Vol. 19. 2001. PP. 99-118
[TAKATSUKA / JARVIS 2001]

199. K.K. TRUONG / R.M. MERSEREAU: Structural Image Codebooks and the Self-Organizing Featur Map Algorithm. In: Proceedings of the International Conference on Acoustics, Speech, and Signal Processing (ICASSP'90), April 1990. Vol. 4. 1990. PP. 2289-92
[TRUONG / MERSEREAU 1990]

200. K.K. TRUONG: Multi-Layer Kohonen Image Codebooks with Logarithmic Search Complexity. In: Proceedings of the International Conference on Acoustics, Speech, and Signal Processing (ICASSP'91). Toronto, Canada, April, 14-17, 1991. Vol. 4. 1991. PP. 2789-92
[TRUONG 1991]

201. Cr. VERSINO / L.M. GAMBARDELLA: Learning Fine Motion in Robotics by Using Hierarchical Neural Networks. IDSIA-5-1995. Technical Report. 1995.
[VERSINO / GAMBARDELLA 1995]

202. Cr. VERSINO / L.M. GAMBARDELLA: Learning Fine Motion by Using the Hierarchical Extended Kohonen Map. In: C. von der MALSBURG et. alt. (Eds.): Proceedings of the 6th International Conference on Artificial Neural Networks (ICANN' 96). Bochum, July 16-19, 1996. Springer-Verl. Berlin u.a. 1996. PP. 221-26
[VERSINO / GAMBARDELLA 1996]

203. J. VESANTO / E. ALHONIEMI / J. HOLLMÉN / O. SIMULA: Monitoring and Modeling of Complex Processes Using Hierarchical Self-Organizing Maps. In: S.-I. AMARI et. alt. (Eds.): Progress in Neural Information Processing. Proceedings of the International Conference on Neural Information. Vol. 2. Springer-Verl. Singapore. 1996. PP. 1169-74 und in: Proceedings of the 1996 IEEE International Symposium on Circuits and Systems (ISCAS'96). Supplement to Vol. 4. 1996. PP. 73-76
[VESANTO / ALHONIEMI / HOLLMÉN / SIMULA 1996]

204. J. VESANTO: Using SOM in Data Mining. Licentiate Thesis. Helsinki University of Technology. Department of Computer Science and Engineering. Espoo, Finland. 2000
[VESANTO 2000]

205. Th. VILLMANN: Topology Preservation in Self-Organizing Maps. In: E. OJA / S. KASKI (Eds.): Kohonen-Maps. Elsevier. Amsterdam u.a. 1999. PP. 279-92
[VILLMANN 1999]

206. Th. VILLMANN / E. MERÉNYI: Extensions and Modifications of the Kohonen-SOM and Applications in Remote Sensing Image Analysis. In: U. SEIFFERT / L.C. JAIN (Eds.): Self-Organizing Neural Networks. Recent Advances and Applications. Physica-Verl. Heidelberg, New York. 2002. PP. 121-42
[VILLMANN / MERÉNYI 2002]

207. N.A. VLASSIS / A. DIMOPOULOS / G. PAPAKONSTANTINOU: The Probabilistic Growing Cell Structures Algorithm. In: W. GERSTNER et. alt. (Eds.): Proceedings of the 7th International Conference on Artificial Neural Networks (ICANN'97). Lausanne, Switzerland, October 8-10, 1997. Springer-Verl. Berlin u.a. 1997. PP. 649-54
[VLASSIS / DIMOPOULOS / PAPAKONSTANTINOU 1997]

208. J.A. WALTER: PSOM Network: Learning with Few Examples. In: Proceedings of the International Conference on Robotics and Automation (ICRA'98). IEEE Service Center. 1998. PP. 2054-59
[WALTER 1998]

209. J.-H. WANG / J.D. RAU / Ch.-Y. PENG: Toward Optimizing a Self-Creating Neural Network. IEEE Transactions on Systems, Man, and Cybernetics. Part B: Cybernetics. Vol. 30. No. 4. 2000. PP. 586-93
[WANG / RAU / PENG 2000]

210. P. WEIERICH / M. v. ROSENBERG: Unsupervised Detection of Driving Sates with Hierarchical Self Organizing Maps. In: M. MARINARO / P.G. MORASSO (Eds.): Proceedings of the International Conference on Artificial Neural Networks (ICANN'94). Vol. 1. Springer-Verl. London/UK. 1994. PP. 246-49
[WEIERICH / v. ROSENBERG 1994.1]

211. P. WEIERICH / M. v. ROSENBERG: The Use of Formal Measures for the Training of Hierarchical Kohonen Maps. In: The IEEE International Conference on Neural Networks (ICNN'94), Orlando, Florida, June 27-29, 1994. IEEE Service Center. Piscataway/NJ. 1994. PP. 612-15
[WEIERICH / v. ROSENBERG 1994.2]

212. T. WEIJTERS: The BP-SOM Architecture and Learning Rule. Neural Processing Letters. Vol. 2. No. 6. 1995. PP. 13-16
[WEIJTERS 1995]

213. T. WEIJTERS / A. Van den BOSCH / H.J. Van den HERIK / E. POSTMA: Avoiding Overfitting with BP-SOM. In: H.J. Van den HERIK / T. WEIJTERS (Eds.): Proceedings of BENELEARN'96. Maastricht. 1996. PP. 157-66
[WEIJTERS / Van den BOSCH / Van den HERIK / POSTMA 1996]

214. T. WEIJTERS / A. Van den BOSCH / H.J. Van den HERIK: Intelligible Neural Networks with BP-SOM. In: Proceedings of the Ninth Dutch Conference on Artificial Intelligence. 1997. PP. 27-36
[WEIJTERS / Van den BOSCH / Van den HERIK 1997.1]

215. T. WEIJTERS / A. Van den BOSCH / H.J. Van den HERIK: Behavioural Aspects of Combining Backpropagation Learning and Self-Organizing Maps. Connection Science. Vol. 9. 1997. PP. 235-52
[WEIJTERS / Van den BOSCH / Van den HERIK 1997.2]

216. T. WEIJTERS / A. Van den BOSCH: Interpretable Neural Networks with BP-SOM. In: J. MIRA et. alt. (Eds.): Tasks and Methods in Applied Artificial Intelligence. Proceedings of the 11th International Conference on Industrial and Engineering Applications of Artificial Intelligence and Expert Systems (IEA'98'AIE). Springer-Verl. Berlin. PP. 564-73
[WEIJTERS / Van den BOSCH 1998]

217. T. WEIJTERS / A. Van den BOSCH / H.J. Van den HERIK: Interpretable Neural Networks with BP-SOM. In: Proceedings of ECML'98. 1998.
[WEIJTERS / Van den BOSCH / Van den HERIK 1998]

218. W.X. WEN / H. LIU / A. JENNINGS: Self-Generating Neural Networks. In: Proceedings of the International Joint Conference on Neural Networks (IJCNN'92), Baltimore, Maryland, June 1992. Vol. 3. 1992.
[WEN / LIU / JENNINGS 1992]

219. W.X. WEN / V. PANG / A. JENNINGS: Self-Generating vs. Self-Organizing, What's Different? In: IEEE International Conference on Neural Networks (ICNN'1993). Vol. 3. San Francisco, California, March 28 – April 1, 1993. 1993. PP. 1469-73
[WEN / PANG / JENNINGS 1993]

220. H. YE / B.W.N. LO: A Visualized Software Library: Nested Self-Organising Maps for Retrieving and Browsing Reusable Software Assets. Neural Computing and Applications. Vol. 9. No. 4. 2000. PP. 266-79
[YE / LO 2000]

221. A. ZELL: Simulation neuronaler Netze. R. Oldenbourg Verl. München, Wien. 1997
[ZELL 1997]

222. B. ZHANG / M. FU / H. YAN / M.A. JABRI: Handwritten Digit Recognition by Adaptive-Subspace Self-Organizing Map (ASSOM). IEEE Transactions on Neural Networks. Vol. 10. No. 4. 1999. PP. 939-45
[ZHANG / FU / YAN / JABRI 1999]
223. Ch.-X. ZHANG / D.A. MLYNSKI: Mapping and Hierarchical Self-Organizing Neural Networks for VLSI Placement. IEEE Transactions on Neural Networks. Vol. 8. No. 2. 1997. PP. 299-314
[ZHANG / MLYNSKI 1997]
224. J.M. ZURADA: Introduction to Artificial Neural Systems. West Publishing Company. 1992
[ZURADA 1992]

ABKÜRZUNGVERZEICHNIS

a.A., A.A.	andere Ansicht, anderer Ansicht
A.d.V.	Anmerkung des Verfassers
bzw.	beziehungsweise
d.b.	das bedeutet
d.f.	daraus folgt
d.h.	das heißt
ders., Ders.	derselbe
dt.	deutsch
engl.	englisch
Fn.	Fußnote
griech.	griechisch
h.M.	herrschende Meinung
i.B.a.	in Bezug auf
i.d.R.	in der Regel
i.S.(v.)	im Sinne (von)
Jhdt.	Jahrhundert
lat.	lateinisch
m.E., M.E.	meines Erachtens
m.a.W.	mit anderen Worten
m.B.a.	mit Bezug auf
s., S.	siehe, Siehe
sgn.	sogenannte, sogenannten, sogenannter
s.v.w.	so viel wie
u.z.	und zwar
v.a.	vor allem
vs.	versus
z.B.	zum Beispiel

0. PROLOG UND MOTIVATION

Das Thema dieser Studienarbeit besteht in der systematischen Darstellung der Architekturtypvarianten von Kohonen-Karten, wobei eine Strukturierung in folgende Kapitel vorgenommen wird:
1. Basaler Architekturtyp: (Basic) Self-Organizing (Feature) Map (SOM) nach T. KOHONEN
2. Architekturtypvariante I: Growing SOM Variants
3. Architekturtypvariante II: Multilevel SOM Variants
4. Architekturtypvariante III: Growing Hierarchical SOM Variants
5. Architekturtypvariante IV: Adaptive Subspace Self-Organizing Map (ASSOM) nach T. KOHONEN et. alt.
6. Architekturtypvariante V: Alternative SOM Variants
7. Kritik und Evaluation.

Die Motivation zu dieser Studienarbeit besteht darin, daß das Standard SOM – Modell in der Literatur aufgrund von Problemen im praktischen Einsatz kritisiert worden ist, u.a. auch was die Thematik der Netzwerktopologie betrifft, weshalb verschiedene Modellvarianten entwickelt worden sind, aus denen etwa siebzig vorgestellt werden.

Ausgehend von der Kohonen-Bibliographie mit ca. 5400 Artikeln, aufrufbar unter http://www.cis.hut.fi/research/som-bibl/ oder einsehbar in S. KASKI / J. KANGAS / T. KOHONEN: Bibliography of Self-Organizing Map (SOM) Papers: 1981-1997. Neural Computing Surveys. Vol. 1. 1998. PP. 102-350 und in M. OJA / S. KASKI / T. KOHONEN: Bibliography of Self-Organizing Map (SOM) Papers: 1998 - 2001 Addendum. Neural Computing Surveys. Vol. 3. 2003. PP. 1-156, wurden unter Hinzuziehung der neueren Artikel von 2001 - 2005 in den Homepages der relevanten Autoren schätzungsweise insgesamt 6000 Artikel, daneben auch einige Monographien, gesichtet und davon etwa 200 Artikel ausgewählt. Dabei wird wie folgt zitiert: Der Autor wird in den Endnoten mit der Angabe des Erscheinungsjahrs und der Seitenangabe des Zitats angegeben, die auf das Literaturverzeichnis verweist. Sofern sowohl der (die) Autor(-en) wie auch das Jahr identisch sein sollte(-n), erfolgt eine an das Jahr angefügte ansteigende Nummer, z.B. verweist „Kohonen 1982.3: 115-17" auf den Artikel des Literaturverzeichnisses:
80. T. KOHONEN: Clustering, Taxonomy, and Topological Maps of Patterns. Proceedings of the 6th International Conference of Pattern Recognition, Munich. 1982. PP. 114-28
[KOHONEN 1982.3].

Die Kapiteleinteilung orientiert sich dabei vor allem an T. KOHONEN[1] und an R.T. FREEMAN und H. YIN[2], daneben auch an S. KASKI[3], J. SI, S. LIN und M.-A. VUONG[4], P.N. SUGANTHAN[5] und J. VESANTO[6].

1. BASALER ARCHITEKTURTYP: (BASIC) SELF-ORGANIZING (FEATURE) MAP (SO(F)M) NACH T. KOHONEN

1.1 Die „Selbstorganisierende (Merkmals-)Karte" (engl.„Self-Organizing (Feature) Map (SOM))" nach dem finnischen Ingenieur Teuvo KOHONEN in ihrer grundlegenden Gestalt (engl.„the basic SOM"[7]) erzeugt einen Ähnlichkeitsgraphen (engl.„similarity graph") aus Eingabedaten, d.h. eine unüberwachte (engl.„unsupervised") Klassifikation von Daten mit topologie- und verteilungserhaltenden Abbildungseigenschaften. Sie bildet die nichtlinearen statistischen Beziehungen zwischen hochdimensionalen Daten ab in einfache geometrische Beziehungen ihrer Bildpunkte auf ein niedrigdimensionales „Array", gewöhnlich ein regelmäßiges zweidimensionales Gitter von Knoten[8]. T. KOHONEN selbst empfiehlt in der Regel „aus Gründen der besseren visuellen Inspektion"[9] eine hexagonale gegenüber einer quadratischen Gitterstruktur und eine rechteckige gegenüber einer quadratischen Gitterform, „damit es für die Karte weniger Symmetrien in der Orientierung gibt. Bei einer runden Karte gäbe es keine stabile Orientierung, bei länglichen Formen ist die Orientierung für die Karte einfacher"[9]. T. KOHONEN selbst macht aber auch Ausnahmen, wobei er nur spärliche Hinweise darüber gibt, welche alternativen Neuronenstrukturen in einem bestimmten Fall vorzuziehen sind bzw. welche Vor- und Nachteile damit einhergehen:

„The lattice type of the array can be defined to be rectangular, hexagonal, or even irregular; hexagonal is effective for visual display."[10]

„Form of the Array. For visual inspection, the hexagonal lattice is to be preferred, because it does not favor horizontal and vertical directions as much as the rectangular array. The edges of the array ought to be rectangular rather than square, because the 'elastic network' formed of the refence vectors m_i must be oriented along with $p(x)$ and be stabilized in the learning process. Notice that if the array were, e.g., circular, it would have no stable orientation in the data space; so any oblongated form is to be preferred. On the other hand, since the m_i have to approximate $p(x)$, it would be desirable to find such dimensions for the array that roughly correspond to the major dimensions of $p(x)$. Therefore, visual inspection of the rough form of $p(x)$, (...) ought to be done first."[11]

„Cyclic Maps. Also cyclic, e.g. toroidal two-dimensional arrays may sometimes be used, especially if it can be concluded that the data are cyclic, too."[12]

„Fixed Grid Topologies. The two basic grid alternatives are: a grid with open edges, which is the structure mainly discussed in this book, and a cyclic network (e.g. sphere or toroid). The toroidal structure, where the horizontal and vertical edges of a square grid are joined cyclically has been used 1. for problems where the data are supposed to be cyclic, e.g., in musical harmonies (...), or 2. when the SOM is used to represent process states. Notice that in a cyclic SOM there are no boundary effects, and all models are in a symmetric position with respect to their neighbors (neighboring states). While the open-edged network corresponds to a single-sheet 'elastic network' that is fitted through the data distribution, the 'elastic network' in the toroidal grid topology corresponds to a double sheet that is similarly fitted to data. A minor drawback is then that in a cyclic grid, some states which are adjacent in the input space may become mapped on opposite sides of the grid.

Of the two trivial alternatives for network topology, viz. the rectangular and the hexagonal grid, the latter is always to be preferred due to its better isotropy."[13] Der SOM-Algorithmus wird am besten von T. KOHONEN[14] selbst beschrieben. Das Modell T. KOHONEN's besteht in der Regel aus einer zweidimensionalen topologischen Anordnung von formalen Neuronen. Jedes formale Neuron i stellt eine (Berechnungs-)Einheit dar, der ein n-dimensionaler sgn.„Gewichts-", „Synapsen-" oder „Referenzvektor" m_i zugeordnet ist, wobei die numerischen Vektorkomponenten zufällig belegt werden (sgn.„Initialisierung"). Alle Neuronen der Eingabeschicht (engl.„input layer") sind mit allen Neuronen der Wettbewerbsschicht (engl.„competitive layer"), auch als sgn.„Kohonen-Schicht" bezeichnet, durch Gewichtsvektoren verknüpft, d.h. alle Wettbewerbsneuronen empfangen die gleichen Eingabesignale, n-dimensionale Vektoren aus dem Eingabevektorraum V. Nun wählt man daraus entsprechend der Wahrscheinlichkeitsdichtefunktion $p(x)$ einen zufälligen Vektor $x = [\xi_1, \xi_2, ..., \xi_n]^T \in IR^n$, der mit allen Referenzvektoren $m_i = [\mu_{i1}, \mu_{i2}, ..., \mu_{in}]^T \in IR^n$ verglichen wird (sgn.„Stimuluswahl"). Die Ansprache, d.h. „Erregung" der einzelnen Wettbewerbsneuronen auf ein gegebenes Eingabesignal ist verschieden stark und wird bestimmt durch die Ähnlichkeit zwischen dem Eingabevektor x und dem jeweiligen Referenzvektor m_i in Bezug auf ein geeignetes (Distanz-)Maß, in der Regel die sgn.„Euklidische Distanz", gekennzeichnet durch $\| \cdot \|$. Je ähnlicher also der Eingabevektor dem entsprechenden Referenzvektor ist, desto stärker wird das zugehörige Neuron „erregt", m.a.W. das sgn.„Erregungszentrum" (engl.„location of the 'response'") bzw. das sgn. „Gewinnerneuron" c (engl.„best-matching node") wird definiert durch die minimalste euklidische Differenz zwischen dem Eingabevektor und den jeweiligen Referenzvektoren.[15] Abschließend wird nun, nachdem das Neuron mit dem am besten übereinstimmenden Referenzvektor bestimmt worden ist, an diesem Neuron und seinen topologischen „Nachbarn" die Übereinstimmung noch erhöht, indem eine Veränderung des Referenzvektors und dessen Nachbarvektoren in Richtung des aktuellen Eingabevektors um einen Bruchteil der gesamten Differenz erfolgt, bestimmt durch die zeitlich veränderliche Lernrate $\alpha(t)$ (engl.„learning-rate factor") im Rahmen der sgn.„Nachbarschaftsfunktion" h_{ci} (engl.„neighborhood function"), m.a.W. das Gewinnerneuron „erregt" andere Neuronen innerhalb einer bestimmten Umgebung und „hemmt" weiter entfernt liegende nach dem sgn.„Prinzip der lateralen Inhibition", sodaß es, das ohnehin von allen Referenzvektoren der Neuronen der Kohonen-Schicht dem Eingangsvektor am ähnlichsten ist, und einige Neuronen in seinem Umfeld dem Eingangsmuster noch um einen gewissen Betrag angenähert wird (sgn.„Adaptation(-s(-lern-)schritt)")[16]:

„The SOM was originally introduced for vectorial input data, and the mapping algorithm was defined as an incremental, stepwise correction process, which is still used in most SOM publications. If $x(t)$ is an n-dimensional vectorial input item identified by the variable t (a running index of the samples, and also the index of the iteration step), and if $\{m_i(t)\}$ is a spatially ordered set of vectorial models arranged as a grid, where i is the index of the node (grid point), then the original SOM algorithm reads:

Step 1. Define the $m_i(t)$ closest to $x(t)$:

$$c = \arg\min_i \{\|x(t) - m_i(t)\|\}. \qquad (1.1)$$

 It is customary to call the best-matching node the winner. In this algorithm the winner is found by direct comparison of x(t) with all the $m_i(t)$; in special adaptive networks (...) the function for the determination of c is called the winner-take-all (WTA) function.
Step 2. Correct the $m_c(t)$ and the $m_i(t)$ in the neighborhood of $m_c(t)$ on the grid towards $x(t)$:

$$m_i(t+1) = m_i(t) + h_{ci}(t)[x(t) - m_i(t)]. \qquad (1.2)$$

 Here $h_{ci}(t)$ is called the neighborhood function. It is similar to a smoothing kernel that has its maximum at the grid point i = c and its value decreases monotonically with increasing spatial distance between grid points i and c. Also h_{ci} usually decreases monotonically with the sample index t, and becomes narrower."[17]
 Die Menge aller Punkte aus dem Eingabevektorraum V, die das gleiche Erregungszentrum c haben, bildet ein Polygon F_c, das sgn.„Voronoipolygon", wobei die Gesamtheit der Voronoipolygone eine Parkettierung oder Partitionierung des Eingaberaums ergibt, die sgn.„Voronoiteilung" oder „-zerlegung" (engl.„Voronoi tesselation"). Das Ziel des KOHONEN-Algorithmus besteht nun darin, eine Belegung der Referenzvektoren m_i zu finden derart, daß die sich ergebende Abbildung vom Eingabevektorraum V auf die topologische Struktur A folgende zwei Eigenschaften besitzt, u.z., erstens, die Topologieerhaltung, d.h. ähnliche Eingabevektoren sollen auf benachbarte oder die gleichen formalen Neuronen in der Struktur A abgebildet werden, sodaß benachbarte Elemente in der Struktur A auch ähnliche Referenzvektoren besitzen, und, zweitens, die Verteilungserhaltung, d.h. die Gebiete des Eingaberaums V mit einer hohen Wahrscheinlichkeitsdichte p(x) sollen auf entsprechend große Bereiche in der Struktur A abgebildet werden, sodaß sich die relative Dichte der Referenzvektoren in A an die Wahrscheinlichkeitsdichte p(x) annähert.[18] [19]
 Abschließend ist noch zu erwähnen, daß etwa zeitgleich ähnliche (Selbstorganisations-)Modelle entwickelt worden waren, u.z. die sgn.„Adaptive Resonance Theory" (ART) von St. GROSSBERG[20] und von Chr. von der Malsburg[21], der, zusammen mit D.J. WILLSHAW, einen Sortieralgorithmus vorgeschlagen hat, der das Wachstum des optischen Nervs beschreibt.
1.2 Diverse Varianten des SOM-Algorithmus werden von T. KOHONEN selbst im Überblick nur kurz vorgestellt, u.z. „Growing SOMs" oder „Dynamically Defined Topologies"[22], „Tree-Search SOM" oder „Tree-Structured SOM"[23], „Cyclic Maps"[24], und „Hierarchical Maps"[25], desweiteren ausführlich „Adaptive-Subspace SOM (ASSOM)[26], die im einzelnen in Kpt. 5 behandelt wird.
1.3 Eine kurze Darstellung der speziellen Probleme des SOM-Algorithmus findet sich in T. KOHONEN: Overture. In: U. SEIFFERT / L.C. JAIN (Eds.): Self-Organizing Neural Networks. Recent Advances and Applications.[27]
1.4 Ein kurzer Überblick über die Vielzahl der Anwendungen bietet T. KOHONEN: Overture. In: U. SEIFFERT / L.C. JAIN (Eds.): Self-Organizing Neural Networks. Recent Advances and Applications.[28]

1.5 Zum Thema „Neural Computing" und „Connectionism" wird verwiesen auf T. KOHONEN: Self-Organizing and Associative Memory.[29]
1.6 Ein Überblick über die SOM-Literatur gibt T. KOHONEN in: Self-Organizing Maps.[30]

2. ARCHITEKTURTYPVARIANTE I: GROWING SOM VARIANTS

Sgn.„growing or incremental network models"[31] besitzen keine von vornherein festgelegte und unveränderliche Netzform, vielmehr werden diese Modelle durch eine aufeinanderfolgende Hinzufügung und Entfernung von Elementen erzeugt. Mit R.T. FREEMAN / H. YIN[32] gibt es zwei unterschiedliche Typen von sgn. „growing SOM variants": Die eine Typvariante wächst ausgehend von einer festen, zumeist rechteckigen Gitterstruktur und -form (Typvariante I.I), wohingegen bei der anderen kein solches festes Gitter verwendet wird, u.z. in der Regel eine dreieckige Netzstruktur, die beliebig angepaßte Netzformen annehmen kann (Typvariante I.II).

2.1 TYPVARIANTE I.I: GROWING ON A FIXED ((HYPER-)RECTANGULAR) GRID

2.11 GROWING GRID (GG) NACH B. FRITZKE

Grundlegend für die Typvariante I.I ist die sgn.„Growing Grid (GG)"- Methode B. FRITZKE's[33], wonach die Netzwerkstruktur ein (hyper-)rechtwinkliges Gitter mit einer bestimmten Dimensionalität k ist und die Startkonfiguration ein k-dimensionaler Hyperkubus (engl.„hypercube") ist, z.B. ein 2 + 2-Gitter für $k = 2$ und ein 2 × 2 × 2-Gitter für $k = 3$.[34] Die Adaptation der Synapsen- oder Referenzvektoren vollzieht sich im Prinzip wie in KOHONEN's SOM-Modell. Die Netzwerkstruktur im GG-Modell erhöht nun aber ihre Größe während der Selbstorganisation, indem ganze Reihen und Spalten von Einheiten anhand einer sgn.„Resourcenvariablen" (engl.„resource variable") eingefügt werden, sodaß das Netzgitter sein Höhe/Breite-Verhältnis der gegebenen Musterverteilung anpassen kann:

„The networks we consider consist of a rectangular $k × m$ grid A of units:
$$A = [a_{ij}], \quad 1 \le i \le k, \quad 1 \le j \le m. \quad (1)"[35]$$

„Each unit $c \in A$ has an associated n-dimensional reference vector w_c denoting the input the unit is maximally tuned to. Moreover, a resource variable τ_c is associated with each unit and is set to 0 initially. The resource variables are used to gather statistical information to decide where to insert new rows or columns of units in the network (...).‟[36]

„At each adaptation step the resource variable of the best-matching unit is incremented
$$\tau_s = \tau_s + 1 \quad (5)$$
and, therefore, these values show how often a unit has been best-matching unit.‟[37]

„For a network of size $k × m$ we perform $k × m × \lambda_g$ adaptation steps before inserting new units. Thus, the parameter λ_g indicates how many adaptation steps on average are done per unit before new units are inserted.
After $k × m × \lambda_g$ number of adaptation steps have been performed, we determine the unit q with maximum resource value:
$$\tau_q \ge \tau_c \quad (\forall c \in A). \quad (6)$$
This unit has been best-matching unit most often and, in order to distribute the signals more evenly over all units, it makes sense to insert a new row or

column in its vicinity. Since there are several possibilities how to do this we have to choose a particular one. We propose to identify the neighbor *f* of *q* with the most different reference vector and to insert a new row (or column) between *q* and *f*. The reasoning behind this choice is that *f* presumably indicates a direction with high variance in the underlying data. This, again, should be taken into account by increasing the resolution of the grid in this direction."[37]

Der Kernpunkt des Verfahrens besteht also darin, daß eine neue Reihe oder Spalte zwischen dem (Gewinner-)Neuron mit dem sgn."maximalen Resourcenwert" (engl."maximum resource value") und seinem Nachbarneuron, das, verglichen mit ihm, den unähnlichsten Referenzvektor besitzt, eingefügt wird, was darauf hindeutet, daß in dieser Richtung eine hohe Variation (engl. "variance") in den zugrunde liegenden Daten vorliegt.

Der Wachstumsvorgang wird fortgesetzt bis die erlaubte Anzahl von Einheiten erreicht ist, oder sofern ein anwendungsbezogenes Kriterium erfüllt ist, z.B., wenn für jedes Neuron im Netzwerk der Anteil der Eingangssignale unter einen bestimmten Grenzwert fällt.[38] In einer abschließenden Approximationsphase (engl."approximation phase") erfolgt dann eine Feinabstimmung der Referenzvektoren während einer Anzahl von Anpassungsschritten mittels einer zeitlich abnehmenden Lernrate.[39]

2.12 GROWING SELF-ORGANIZING MAP (GSOM) NACH H.-U. BAUER / Th. VILLMANN

Der sgn."Growing Self-Organizing Map (GSOM)"- Ansatz H.-U. BAUER's und Th. VILLMANN's[40] erzeugt, ausgehend von einer bestehenbleibenden regelmäßigen Gitterstruktur A, einen (rechteckigen) Hyperkubus, einen verbesserten Grad an Topologieerhaltung im Vergleich zur Standard-SOM, indem eine (Gitter-)Strukturadaptation (engl."structure adaptation") stattfindet, d.h., entweder wird die (Gesamt-)Dimensionalität des Hyperkubus oder das Längenverhältnis zwischen seinen verschiedenen (Gitter-)Dimensionen variabel an die Eingaberaumtopologie angepasst[41]:

„The GSOM starts from an initial 2-neuron configuration, learns according to the regular SOM-algorithm, adds neurons to the output space with respect to a certain criterion to be described below, learns again, adds again, etc., until a prespecified maximum number N_{max} of neurons is distributed. During this procedure, the output space topology remains to be of the form $n_1 \times n_2 \times \ldots$, with $n_j = 1$ for $j > D_A$, where D_A is the current dimensionality of A. Hence, the initial configuration is $2 \times 1 \times 1 \ldots$, $D_A = 1$. From there it can grow either by adding nodes in one of the directions which are already spanned by the output space, i.e. by having $n_i \rightarrow n_i + 1$, $i \leq D_A$, or by adding a new dimension, i.e. $(n_{D_{A+1}} = 1) \rightarrow (n_{D_{A+1}} = 2)$, $D_A \rightarrow D_A + 1 (\ldots)$.

The decision in which direction nodes have to be added or whether a new direction has to be initialized is made on the basis of the receptive fields Ω_r"[42], i.e. „on the basis of the fluctuations within the masked Voronoi cells of the neurons. The masked Voronoi cell $\Omega_r \subseteq V$ is the subset of data points $v \in$

$V \subseteq R^{d_v}$ which are mapped onto node r."[43]

„When reconstructing v ∈ V from neuron r, an error

$$\theta = v - w_r = \sum_{i=1}^{D_A} a_i(v)\frac{w_{r+e_i} - w_{r-e_i}}{\left\| w_{r+e_i} - w_{r-e_i}\right\|} + v',\ v' = a_{D_{A+1}}(v)\frac{\omega_{PCA}}{\left\|\omega_{PCA}\right\|} + v'' \qquad (4.1)$$

remains decomposed along the different directions, which result from projecting back the output space grid into the input space V (...). Thereby, e_i denotes the unit vector in direction i of A. (...) Considering the receptive field Ω_r and determining their first principle component ω_{PCA} allows a further decomposition of v'. Projection of v' onto the direction of ω_{PCA} then yields $a_{D_{A+1}}(v)$ in (4.1).

The criterion for the growing now is to add nodes in that direction which has on average the largest error (normalized) expected amplitudes $\bar{a}_i$:

$$\bar{a}_i = \sqrt{\frac{n_i}{n_i+1}} \sum_v \frac{|a_i(v)|}{\sqrt{\sum_{j=1}^{D_A+1} a_j^2(v)}},\quad i = 1,...,D_A+1 \qquad (4.2)$$

Once a direction in which to grow has been determined, new nodes have to be initialized. After each growth step, a new learning phase has to take place, in order to readjust the map."[44]

Der Kernpunkt des Verfahrens besteht also darin, daß im Rahmen der Rekonstruktion (engl.„reconstructing") der Eingabedatenpunkte aus dem betreffenden (Gitter-)Neuron im Sinne einer Rückprojektion (engl.„backprojecting") ein sgn.(„Rekonstruktions-)Fehler" (engl.„reconstruction error") verbleibt, der in die verschiedenen (Dimensions-)Richtungen zerlegt wird, wobei nun das Kriterium zur Bestimmung der richtigen Wachstumsrichtung darin liegt, ein Neuron in die Richtung hinzuzufügen, die im Durchschnitt den größten sgn.„Fehlerumfang" (engl.„error amplitude") aufweist.

2.13 INCREMENTAL GRID GROWING (IGG) NACH R. MIIKKULAINEN / J. BLACK-MORE UND (GROWING) LATERALLY INTERCONNECTED SYNERGETICALLY SELF-ORGANIZING MAPS ((G)LISSOM) NACH R. MIIKKULAINEN / J.A. BEDNAR / A. KELKAR / J. SIROSH ET. ALT.

Dem sgn.„Incremental Grid Growing (IGG)"- Modell R. MIIKKULAINEN's und J. BLACKMORE's[45] liegt eine stets regelmäßige 2-dimensionale, viereckige Gitterstruktur zugrunde, die mit vier Knoten initialisiert wird. Ein Knoten wird nun in solchen Gebieten am Rande des Gitters hinzugefügt, wenn es das entsprechende Eingabegebiet inadäquat repräsentiert, d.h., wann immer ein Grenzknoten (engl.„boundary node") zum Gewinnerneuron wird, erhöht sich der Wert seines sgn.„(an-)gehäuften Fehlers" (engl.„cumulative error")

$$E(t) = E(t-1) + \sum_k (x_k - w_k)^2,$$

wobei am Ende jeder Iteration der Grenzknoten mit dem größten gehäuften

Fehler, der demnach am unangemessensten (engl.„most inadequately")
das Gebiet des entsprechenden Eingaberaums darstellt, als sgn.„Fehlerkno-
ten" (engl.„error node") bezeichnet wird und von dem aus neue Knoten an
alle unbesetzten Gitterstellen in seiner unmittelbaren Nachbarschaft „wachsen", die dann mit ihm verbunden werden. Außerdem können neue Verbindungen hinzugefügt werden, falls während der Netzorganisation neue Neuronen entstehen, deren Gewichtsvektoren sich denen ihrer Nachbarn annä-
hern, mit denen sie noch nicht verbunden sind.[46]
 Hinzuweisen wäre noch auf das sgn.„(Growing) Laterally Interconnected
Synergetically Self-Organizing Maps ((G)LISSOM)"- Modell R. MIIKKULAINEN's,
J.A. BEDNAR's, A. KELKAR's, J. SIROSH's et. alt.[47], wobei – in Analogie zum GG-
Modell B. FRITZKE's – ebenfalls ganze Reihen und Spalten von Neuronen neu
hinzugefügt werden, um, basierend auf dem sgn.„Receptive - Field Laterally
Interconnected Synergetically Self-Organizing Map (RF-LISSOM)"- Modell, die
topographische Organisation und die funktionalen Eigenschaften der Retina
und des visuellen Cortex zu modellieren.

2.131 GROWING LEXICAL MAP (GLM) NACH I. FARKAS / P. LI

Dem IGG-Modell ähnlich ist das sgn.„Growing Lexical Map (GLM)" von
I. FARKAS und P. LI[48] in der Lage, sich ein wachsendes „Wörterbuch" (engl.
„lexicon") anzueignen.

2.14 GROWING (OR DYNAMIC) SELF-ORGANIZING MAP (GSOM) NACH D. ALAHA-KOON / S.K. HALGAMUGE / B. SRINIVASAN / A.L. HSU / ET. ALT.

Einige Charakteristiken, ähnlich zum IGG-Konzept, besitzt das sgn.„Growing
Self-Organizing Map (GSOM)"- Modell von D. ALAHAKOON, S.K. HALGAMU-
GE, B. SRINIVASAN, A.L. HSU et. alt.[49] Die GSOM-Gitterstruktur ist dieselbe wie
im IGG-Konzept, und der Fehlerwert des Gewinnerknotens wird ebenfalls erhöht. Das „Knotenwachstum" wird initiiert, wenn der Wert des Gesamtfehlers
(engl.„total error (TE)") eines (Grenz-)Knotens den sgn.„growth threshold
(GT)" (dt.„Wachstumsschwellenwert") überschreitet, d.h. $TE_i \geq GT$:

$$TE_i = \sum_{H_i} \sum_{j=1}^{D} (x_{i,j} - w_j)^2, \quad \text{und} \quad GT = -D \times \ln(SF),$$

wobei H die Anzahl der „Treffer" (engl.„hits") des Knotens i, D die Dimension
der Daten und der Parameter SF den sgn.„spread factor" (dt.„Spannfaktor")
darstellt.[50]

2.15 GROWING (OR DYNAMIC) SELF-ORGANIZING MAP (GSOM) NACH A.L. HSU / S.K. HALGAMUGE

Um die topographischen Qualitäten des GSOM-Algorithmus zu steigern, wird
von A.L. HSU und S.K. HALGAMUGE[51] eine hexagonale Gitterstruktur verwendet, wobei jetzt mit sieben Knoten initialisiert wird. Ferner wird das sgn.„Moving Average Directed Growing (MADG)"- Verfahren[52] oder das „Recursive

Means Directed Growing (RMDG)"- Verfahren[53], wie es von T. KOHONEN genannt worden ist, eingeführt, um topographische Verzerrungen, verursacht durch neu eingefügte Knoten, zu verhindern.

2.16 GROWING SELF-ORGANIZING MAP NACH A. NÜRNBERGER ET. ALT.

Ebenfalls auf dem GSOM-Algorithmus D. ALAHAKOON's et. alt. basierend ist der sgn.„Growing Self-Organizing Map Approach" von A. NÜRNBERGER[54], der ebenfalls mit einer hexagonalen Kartenstruktur arbeitet.

2.17 GROWING SELF-ORGANIZING MAP (GSOM) NACH J. MONNERJAHN

Aufbauend auf dem sgn.„Resizing Algorithm"- Verfahren, das es erlaubt, eine trainierte KOHONEN-Karte in eine andere Größe zu transformieren, wird von J. MONNERJAHN[55] ein rechteckiges sgn.„Growing Self-Organizing Map (GSOM)" - Modell vorgestellt, das entweder bis zu einer vorbestimmten Netzwerkgröße wachsen kann oder – in Analogie zum GG-Model B. FRITZKE's – seine geeignete Größe und sein Höhe/Breite-Verhältnis bezüglich einer gegebenen Eingabeverteilung selbst finden kann.

2.18 STRUCTURE-ADAPTIVE SOM WITH DYNAMICAL NODE SPLITTING SCHEME NACH S.B. CHO

Bei der sgn.„Structure-Adaptive SOM with Dynamical Node Splitting Scheme" von S.B. CHO[56], wird eine quadratische Gitterstruktur von 4×4 Knoten zur Mustererkennung von handgeschriebenen Buchstaben verwendet, wobei, wenn ein Knoten mehr als eine Klasse repräsentiert, dieser durch eine Subkarte (engl.„submap"), bestehend aus vier Knoten, ersetzt wird.

2.191 GROWING MULTI-DIMENSIONAL SELF-ORGANIZING MAP UND QUASI-FOUR-DIMENSIONAL-NEURONCUBE (QFDN) NACH U. SEIFFERT / B. MICHAELIS ET. ALT.

Das sgn.„Growing Multi-Dimensional Self-Organizing Map"- Konzept nach U. SEIFFERT und B. MICHAELIS et. alt.[57] behandelt das Problem der ortsunabhängigen Klassenbildung im Rahmen der Bildverarbeitung, wobei ebenfalls ein sgn.„error value" darüber entscheidet, wann eine Reihe oder Spalte von neuen Neuronen einzufügen ist.

2.192 SPACE PARTITION NETWORK (SPAN) NACH Ts.-Ch. LEE / A.M. PETERSON

Das sgn.„Space Partition Network (SPAN)"- Modell Ts.-Ch. LEE's und A.M. PETERSON's[58], die Basis bildend für ein flexibles und adaptives Signalrepräsentationssystem, besitzt eine rechtwinklige Gitterstruktur und verwendet den „quantization error" als das Maß, um zu bestimmen, wann ein neues Neuron zu generieren ist.

2.193 INTERPOLATIVE ALGORITHM NACH J.S. RODRIGUES / L.B. ALMEIDA

Das sgn.„Interpolative Algorithm"- Konzept von J.S. RODRIGUES und L.B. AL-
MEIDA[59], benutzt eine rechteckige Neuronenstruktur, die anhand von Inter-
polations(-adaptions-)zyklen auf die gewünschte Größe gebracht wird.

2.194 MORPHOGENETIC ALGORITHM NACH St. JOKUSCH

Das sgn.„Morphogenetic Algorithm"- Konzept St. JOKUSCH's[60], ausgehend
von einer rechteckigen Gitterform, basiert auf dem ART-Modell G. CARPEN-
TER's und St. GROSSBERG's und inspirierte B. FRITZKE nach eigenem Bekunden
zu seinem GCS-Modell.[61]
Um das Erregungszentrum zu ermitteln, wird das Skalarprodukt zwischen
dem normierten Eingabe- und Gewichtsvektor gebildet und ein neues Neuron eingefügt, sofern ein Vektor des Eingabemusters auftritt, dessen Skalarprodukt mit dem Gewichtsvektor des Gewinnerneurons einen kritischen
Wert

$$q_{crit}(t)=\hat{q}_{crit}[1-\exp(\frac{t-t^{new}}{\tau})]$$

(engl.„critical match") unterschreitet. Nachdem ein Nachbarneuron des
Gewinnerneurons zufällig ausgesucht worden ist und es sowie seine angren-
zenden Neuronen um eine Gitterposition vom Gewinnerneuron wegge-
schoben worden sind, wird das neue Neuron an seine Stelle in der Gitterstruktur eingefügt.[62]

2.2 TYPVARIANTE I.II: GROWING WITHOUT USING A FIXED GRID

2.21 GROWING CELL STRUCTURES (GCS) NACH B. FRITZKE

Grundlegend für die Typvariante I.II ist das sgn.„Growing Cell Structures
(GCS)" (dt.„Wachsende Zellstrukturen") - Modell B. FRITZKE's.[63] Im Gegensatz
zur KOHONEN-Karte, die „die Elemente einer vorgegebenen Neuronenstruktur adaptiert"[64], läßt sich das GCS-Modell als ein Entwicklungsprozeß interpre-
tieren, der „zu maßgeschneiderten Neuronenstrukturen"[64] in bezug auf die zu
verwirklichende Abbildung der unbekannten Wahrscheinlichkeitsverteilung
$p(\xi)$ der Eingabesignale führt, m.a.W. „eine k-dimensionale Struktur A von
formalen Neuronen (...) wird nicht am Anfang definiert und bleibt dann un-
verändert, stattdessen werden, ausgehend von einer minimalen Initialstruktur, sukzessive Zellen eingefügt und gelöscht, bis eine passende Form gefun-
den ist"[65].
Das GCS-Modell besitzt nun folgende Netzstruktur: „Die verwendeten Grund-
bausteine sind k-dimensionale Simplices" (engl.„simplices"). „Ein k-dimensio-
naler Simplex ist ein topologisches Gebilde mit $k+1$ Ecken, die jeweils paar-
weise durch Kanten verbunden sind. Für $k=1$ ist dies eine Linie, für $k=2$ ein
Dreieck und für $k=3$ ein Tetraeder" (engl.„tetrahedron"). „Bei höheren Dimensionen spricht man von k-dimensionalen Hypertetraedern" (engl.„hy-

pertetrahedrons"). (...) „Im allgemeinen bestehen die Strukturen aus mehreren zusammenhängenden Simplices. Initialstruktur ist stets ein einzelner Simplex. Die Simplexecken sind die Zellen, und die Kanten stehen für Nachbarschaftsbeziehungen."[66]

Die Adaptation der Synapsen- oder Referenzvektoren vollzieht sich im Prinzip wie in KOHONEN's SOM-Modell. Die Netzwerkdynamik des GCS-Modells erlaubt nun ferner das Einfügen von neuen Zellen: „Jeweils nach einer festen Anzahl λ von Adaptionsschritten wird eine neue Zelle in die Struktur eingefügt. (...)

Ein Ziel des Selbstorganisationsprozesses ist nach Voraussetzung die Modellierung der unbekannten Wahrscheinlichkeitsverteilung $P(\xi)$ durch die Verteilung der Referenzvektoren w_i. Dieses Ziel ist für eine gegebene Netzkonfiguration dann erreicht, wenn jede Zelle die gleiche Chance hat, Erregungszentrum für das nächste Eingabesignal gemäß $P(\xi)$ zu sein. Es muß also gelten:

$$\int_{F_i} p(\xi)\,d\xi = \frac{1}{N} \qquad \text{für alle } i \in A \qquad (7.5)$$

Da $P(\xi)$ i.a. unbekannt ist, können wir die Wahrscheinlichkeit, daß eine bestimmte Zelle c Erregungszentrum wird, nur schätzen, indem wir den Anteil der Signale betrachten, für die c in der Vergangenheit Erregungszentrum gewesen ist.

Für jede Zelle i wird deshalb der lokale Signalzähler τ_i eingeführt, der immer dann um eins erhöht wird, wenn c bei einem Adaptionsschritt Erregungszentrum ist. Damit läßt sich die relative Signalhäufigkeit von i definieren durch

$$h_i := \frac{\tau_i}{\sum_{j \in A} \tau_j} \qquad (7.6)$$

Ziel ist eine gleiche relative Signalhäufigkeit für alle Zellen. Ein hoher Wert von h_i deutet darauf hin, daß das Einzugsgebiet der Zelle i, also das zu ihrem Referenzvektor w_i gehörende Voronoigebiet F_i, zu groß ist. Deshalb bestimmen wir, wenn wir eine Zelle einfügen wollen, die Zelle q mit der Eigenschaft, daß h_q maximal ist, also

$$h_q \geq h_i \quad \text{(bzw. äquivalent)} \quad \tau_q \geq \tau_i \quad (\forall i \in A) \qquad (7.7)$$

Es ist günstig, der neuen einzufügenden Zelle r einen Referenzvektor w_r zu geben, der sehr ähnlich zu w_q ist. Dadurch wird das Einzugsgebiet von q verkleinert, was sehr wahrscheinlich zur Folge hat, daß auch h_q im Laufe der nächsten Zeit kleiner wird.

Nun ist noch die Position der neuen Zelle in der Struktur A festzulegen. Es ist erwünscht, daß in A benachbarte Zellen ähnliche Referenzvektoren haben. Umgekehrt sollen Zellen mit ähnlichen Referenzvektoren auch benachbart in A sein. Deswegen ist es angebracht, die neue Zelle in direkter topologischer Nachbarschaft zu q einzufügen. Wir tun dies im folgenden stets dadurch, daß wir die neue Zelle zwischen q und demjenigen direkten Nachbarn f von q einfügen, dessen Referenzvektor am weitesten entfernt von w_i ist. Dies kann man anschaulich beschreiben als 'Spalten der Kante zwischen q und f'.

Wir bestimmen also f durch

$$\|w_f - w_q\| \geq \|w_i - w_q\| \quad (\forall i \in N_q) \qquad (7.8)$$

und fügen die neue Zelle r zwischen q und f ein. Anschließend wird r so mit den umliegenden Zellen verbunden, daß wieder eine Struktur entsteht, die ausschließlich aus k-dimensionalen Simplices besteht. (...) Der Referenzvektor von r wird initialisiert durch

$$w_r := \frac{w_q + w_f}{2} \qquad (7.9)$$

Die neue Zelle wird auf diese Weise sowohl im Eingaberaum V als auch in der Struktur A zwischen f und q plaziert. Diese geordnete Einfügung sorgt dafür, daß eine geordnete Struktur auch geordnet bleibt. Es können durch eine Einfügung keine topologischen Defekte entstehen."[67]
Der Kernpunkt des Verfahrens besteht also darin, daß die Kante des Simplexes gespalten wird, an dessen Ecken sich das Gewinnerneuron q und sein direktes Nachbarneuron f mit dem unähnlichsten Referenzvektor befindet, die neue Zelle r eingefügt und mit den umliegenden Zellen verbunden wird.[68]
Bei einer Netztopologie für eine strukturierte Wahrscheinlichkeitsverteilung kann es zu langen Verbindungen oder zu einer Reihe von Zellen mit Referenzvektoren kommen, die in Gebieten liegen, in denen die Wahrscheinlichkeitsdichte $p(\xi)$ sehr niedrig oder gleich Null ist, sodaß das Entfernen der Zellen erfolgt, um die Topologie der Eingabedatenverteilung $p(\xi)$ noch besser zu modellieren.[69 70]

2.211 (GROWING) DYNAMIC CELL STRUCTURES ((G)DCS) NACH J. BRUSKE / G. SOMMER ET. ALT.

Das sgn.„(Growing) Dynamic Cell Structures ((G)DCS(-GCS))" - Modell von J. BRUSKE und G. SOMMER et. alt.[71] arbeitet wie das GCS-Modell B. FRITZKE's mit dem Unterschied, daß „the topology of the graph G (lateral connection scheme between the neural units) is not of a predefined and fixed dimensionality k but rather is learned on-line (during training) (...)."[72]

2.212 MULTIPLE GROWING CELL STRUCTURES (MGCS) UND EXTERNALLY GROWING CELL STRUCTURES (EGCS) NACH G. CHENG / A. ZELL

Basierend auf dem GCS - Modell B. FRITZKE's werden im sgn.„Multiple Growing Cell Structures (MGCS)"- Modell von G. CHENG / A. ZELL[73] zugleich mehrere neue Zellen eingefügt, und – in Anlehnung an J. BRUSKE's und G. SOMMER's DCS-Modell – der „Einfügepunkt" (engl.„insertion point") der neuen Zellen auf einer variablen Position vorgenommen wird, was auch für das sgn.„Externally Growing Cell Structures (EGCS)"- Modell[74] gilt, und zusätzlich: „(...) when (...) the Maximum Error Vertex (MEV) is a boundary node, the new cell is grown externally."[75]

2.213 GROWING CELL STRUCTURES NACH W. DENG / W. WU

W. DENG und W. WU[76] präsentieren eine neue Methode der Dokumenten-klassifikation, indem jedes Dokument anhand eines sgn.„microfeature weight vector" repräsentiert wird, wodurch die semantischen Beziehungen zwischen den Dokumenten Berücksichtigung finden und diese dann anhand des GCS-Algorithmus klassifiziert werden.

2.214 SELF-CREATING NEURAL NETWORK NACH J.-H. WANG / J.D. RAU / Ch.-Y. PENG

J.-H. WANG, J.D. RAU und Ch.-Y. PENG[77] versuchen, den GCS-Algorithmus als ein „self-creating model" zu optimieren.

2.215 GROWING AND SPLITTING NEURAL NETWORK NACH D. MERKL / M. KÖHLE

D. MERKL und M. KÖHLE[78] verwenden ein sgn.„Growing and Splitting Neural Network", angelehnt an das GCS-Modell B. FRITZKE's, zur Klassifikation von Dokumenten.

2.22 DYNAMIC TOPOLOGY REPRESENTING NETWORK (DTRN) NACH J. SI / S. LIN / M.-A. VUONG

Im sgn.„Dynamic Topology Representing Network (DTRN)"- Algorithmus J. SI's, S. LIN's und M.-A. VUONG's[79] wird, beginnend mit nur einem Gitterknoten, und, ähnlich wie im ART 2-Modell von G.A. CARPENTER und S. GROSSBERG, ein ständig abnehmender sgn.„vigilance threshold" als Kriterium für das Einfügen von Knoten verwendet:

$$\|X - W_c\| < \rho \quad (\rho: \text{vigilance threshold}) \text{ mit} \quad \rho = \rho_0 \left(\frac{\rho_1}{\rho_0}\right)^{\left(\frac{k}{k_{max}}\right)}$$

Versagt der Gewinnerknoten c den sgn.„vigilance test", wird ein neuer Knoten erzeugt.

2.221 GROWING SELF-ORGANIZING NETWORK WITH ANT CLUSTERING ALGORITHM NACH T. MIKAMI / M. WADA

Der DTRN-Algorithmus J. SI's et. alt. wird von T. MIKAMI und M. WADA[80] zu verbessern versucht, indem er mit anderen Datenvisualisationstechniken integriert wird, basierend auf dem sgn.„Ant Clustering Algorithm"-Verfahren von E. LUMER et. alt.

2.23 GROWING SELF-ORGANIZING ALGORITHM NACH T. SAITO / R. OHTA

Das GCS-Modell B. FRITZKE's verwendend führen T. SAITO und R. OHTA[81] mehrere Experimente durch.

2.24 PROBABILISTIC GROWING CELL STRUCTURES (PGCS) NACH N.A. VLASSIS / A. DIMOPOULOS / G. PAPAKONSTANTINOU

Das sgn.„Probabilistic Growing Cell Structures (PGCS)"- Modell von N.A. VLASSIS, A. DIMOPOULOS / G. PAPAKONSTANTINOU[82] nimmt an, daß in jedem Cluster die Samples anhand einer bekannten sgn.„probability density function" verteilt sind, und ebenso, daß jeder Cluster gegenüber den anderen eine sgn.„a priori Präferenz" mit einer bestimmten Vorzugswahrscheinlichkeit (engl.„prior probability") besitzt, die die Zugehörigkeitswahrscheinlichkeit eines neuen Samples zu einem Cluster bestimmt.

3. ARCHITEKTURTYPVARIANTE II: MULTILEVEL SOM VARIANTS

Sgn.„multilevel" oder „multilayer self-organizing-maps"[83] besitzen eine hierarchische Struktur. Man kann mit T. KOHONEN[84] eine Vielzahl von Varianten unterscheiden, wobei hier zwei grundlegende Typen von sgn.„multilevel SOM variants" behandelt werden: die eine Typvariante ist dadurch gekennzeichnet, daß – in Analogie zu sgn.„multilayer feedforward networks" (dt.„vorwärtsgerichtete Mehrschichtennetzwerke") – mehrere KOHONEN-Schichten oder -ebenen hinter- und nebeneinander angeordnet sind, wobei die Ausgabe der vorangehenden SOM als Eingabe in die nachfolgende SOM eingespeist wird, u.z. derart, daß alle Neuronen der vorhergehenden Schicht mit allen Neuronen der nächsten Schicht verbunden sind (Typvariante II.I), wohingegen bei der anderen Typvariante mehrere SOMs in Form einer (Baum-)Pyramidenstruktur verknüpft sind derart, daß die Verbindungen zwischen den aufeinanderfolgenden SOMs durch das Baumverknüpfungsmuster eingeschränkt sind (Typvariante II.II).

3.1 TYPVARIANTE II.I: HIERARCHICAL SOMS

3.11 HIERARCHICAL SELF-ORGANIZING MAP (HSOM) NACH J. LAMPINEN / E. OJA

Das sgn.„Hierarchical Self-Organizing Map (HSOM)"- Modell von J. LAMPINEN und E. OJA[85], hervorgegangen aus dem sgn.„Hierarchical Vector Quantization"- Modell St. LUTTRELL's (s. Kpt. 3.26), stellt eine Mehrschichten-Version der selbstorganisierenden Karte T. KOHONEN's (engl.„multilayer SOM") dar. Als Clustermethode kann es beliebig komplexe Cluster (dt.„traubenförmige Anordnung" i.S.v. „(Punkt-)Menge" oder „Haufen" i.S.v. „Klassen") bilden, m.a. W. beliebig komplexe Klassengrenzen formen[86], darüberhinaus bietet es ein „natürliches" (engl.„natural") Abstandsmaß eines Punktes zu einem Cluster, das sich der lokalen Statistik der (Eingangs-)Daten anpaßt: „The hierarchical SOM is here defined as a two-dimensional SOM whose operating principle is:
1. For each input vector x, the best matching unit is chosen from the first layer map and its index b is input to the second layer;
2. The best matching unit for b is chosen from the second layer map and its index is the output of the network.
 One thing is immediately clear from the above: because each first-layer map unit i has a convex polyhedral Voronoi region V_i defined by equation (1):

$$\|x-m_b\|=\min\|x-m_j\|, \quad j=1,...,M \quad (1),$$

and each second layer unit j is the best-matching unit for a subset, say $i_1, ..., i_k$ of the first layer indices, the second layer unit is in fact the best-matching unit for any $x \in U^k_{k=1} V_{ik}$. This region is an arbitrary union of non-overlapping convex polyhedral regions. Any region in IR^n can be approximated by such a union to an arbitrary accuracy, when the number of component regions V_{ik} is arbitrarily large. Thus, clusters of arbitrary shapes can be represented by the two-layer map. (...)
 The main advantage of HSOM clustering with respect to classical clustering

methods, e.g. k-means, is the adaptive distance measure. (...)
Compared to the simple linkage clustering the HSOM offers a distance measure that takes into account all the points in the cluster. As can be seen from equation (20), the cost introduced by one data point contains the distance of the point from all the other clusters, weighted by the distance of each cluster along the lattice."[87]
„The cost introduced by one data sample x_p is

$$E'(x_p)=\sum_k h(b(x_p)-k)\|x_p-m_k\|^2. \qquad (20)$$

The cost function $E'(x_p)$ can be interpreted as the distance from the point x_p to the cluster represented by the whole SOM network, and learning tries to minimize the total distance from points to the cluster."[88]
Mit anderen Worten:
„The cost is a weighted distance of the sample from the nearest units along the lattice, and since the units are roughly equiprobable, the neighborhood h always covers roughly equal portion of the input samples."[89]
„In clustering terminology, while the first SOM layer forms one large cluster of all the data samples so that the total distance of the samples from the cluster is minimized, the second map in HSOM then splits the large cluster into equal size parts. Since the distance relations of the data samples are preserved on the map, the cluster numbers or indices of the best matching units can be used as a measure of distance of the original data samples. What is gained by the HSOM is that each high dimensional data vector is mapped to a low dimensional discrete value so that comparing the values implicitly contains comparison of the original distances."[90]

3.12 HIERARCHICAL NEURAL NETWORK NACH Th.M. MARTINETZ / Kl.J. SCHULTEN

Das sgn.„Hierarchical Neural Network" von Th.M. MARTINETZ und Kl.J. SCHULTEN[91], dient der Bewegungssteuerung eines Robotergreifarms, wobei die Netzwerkarchitektur aus einer „Kopplung" (engl.„coupling") eines 3-dimensionalen kubischen Gitters besteht, an welches an jedem Gitterknoten ein 2-dimensionales quadratisches Gitter „angeheftet" ist, sodaß das 3D-Hauptnetz die Armstellung und -bewegung kontrolliert, und das untergeordnete 2D-Netz die Ausrichtung des Greifers, dem an einer zufällig gewählten Stelle ein anhand von zwei Kameras zu sehender Zylinder präsentiert wird: „For the discretization of the space X of input signals x we choose nets of a two-dimensional topology because the orientation of the cylinder has two degrees of freedom, and, therefore, the relevant submanifold of actual input signals x is two-dimensional. For the control of the two angels of the gripper, we assign to each element q of subnet S_s a two-dimensional vector Φ_{qs} for the gross orientation of the gripper and a tensor B_{qs} of dimension 2×4 for subsequent corrective fine movements. After the selection of element s, vector Φ_{qs} and tensor B_{qs} of the discretization point q which is closest to the input x are chosen to perform the orientation of the gripper.
For learning the output values Φ_{qs} and B_{qs}, adaptation steps (...) are employed. First, by a steepest descent learning rule of the Widrow-Hoff type (...) im-

proved estimates Φ* and B* are determined. Since the elements of subnet S_s are again assigned to the input space X in a topologically correct manner, the result can be used to adapt the output values in a whole neighborhood of neuron q (...). Additionally, because the subnets are also arranged in a to-pologically correct way within the three-dimensional grid, the learning suc-cess of neuron q may also be 'spread' to neighboring subnets. Adjacent sub-nets have to learn similar transformations $\Phi_s(x)$, and, therefore, may bene-fit from sharing adjustments of Φ_{qs} and B_{qs}. This hierarchical cooperation be-tween neurons within a subnet and between subnets in the main net can be expressed mathematically by

$$B_{rp}^{new} = B_{rp}^{old} + \epsilon h_{rs} \delta g_{pq}(B^{\xi} - B_{rp}^{old}), \qquad (6)$$

$$\vec{\phi}_{rp}^{new} = \vec{\phi}_{rp}^{old} + \epsilon h_{rs} \delta g_{pq}(\vec{\phi}\xi - \vec{\phi}_{rp}^{old}). \qquad (7)$$

The tensor h_{rs} defines the range of cooperation between subnets (...). The second tensor g_{pq} describes the neighborhood between units within each subnet and is of the same form as h_{rs}, namely unity at p = q and vanishing as the distance between p and q increases. The factor ε and δ scale the size of the adaptation steps and decrease as learning proceeds (...).
This hierarchical cooperation between the neurons and between the sub-nets leads to a significant acceleration of the learning process."[92]

3.13 HIERARCHICAL SELF-ORGANIZING MODEL (HSOM) UND HIERARCHICAL HYBRID NEURAL MODEL (HHNM) NACH O.A.S. CARPINTEIRO ET. ALT.

Das sgn.„Hierarchical Self-Organizing Model (HSOM)" nach O.A.S. CARPINTEI-RO et. alt.[93] macht einen wirksamen Gebrauch von Kontextinformationen, was es befähigt, sequentielle Klassifikationen auszuführen, z.B. von Musikstük-ken. Es setzt sich zusammen aus zwei übereinandergelagerten SOMs, der „bottom-" und der „top-SOM", wobei gilt: „The input to the top SOM is deter-mined by the distance ψ(i,t) of the n units in the map of the bottom SOM."[94] Eine Weiterentwicklung dessen stellt das sgn.„Hierarchical Hybrid Neural Model (HHNM)"[95] dar, das aus dem HSOM und einem ihm nachgeschalteten „single-layer perceptron (SLP)" besteht.

3.14 HIERARCHICAL EXTENDED KOHONEN MAP (HEKM) NACH Cr. VERSINO / L.M. GAMBARDELLA

Das sgn.„Hierarchical Extended Kohonen Map (HEKM)"- Modell von Cr. VER-SINO und L.M. GAMBARDELLA[96] wird verwendet für das sgn.„path finding problem" in der Robotik, bestehend aus einem „super-net", zuständig für den „perception vector", und den untergeordneten „sub-nets", verbunden mit jedem Neuron des „super-net", zuständig für den „2-dimensional relative goal direction vector".

3.15 HIERARCHICAL SELF-ORGANIZING MAP NACH J. VESANTO / E. ALHONIEMI ET. ALT.

Die sgn."Hierarchical SOM"- Konstruktion nach J. VESANTO und E. ALHONIEMI et.alt.[97] modelliert komplexe industrielle Prozesse, wobei sich SOMs auf zwei Ebenen befinden, u.z. die „state map" und die „dynamics maps", die mit jedem Neuron der „state map" verknüpft sind: „The state map can be used to track the operating point of the process being investigated; the dynamics maps are used in prediction of the next state on state map."[98]

3.16 MAPPING AND HIERARCHICAL SELF-ORGANIZING NEURAL NETWORK (MHSO) NACH Ch.-X ZHANG / D.A. MLYNSKI

Ch.-X ZHANG und D.A. MLYNSKI[99] haben einen sgn."Mapping and Hierarchical Self-Organizing Neural Network (MHSO(2)) Algorithm" entwickelt für das „placement problem for VLSI circuits".

3.17 HIERARCHICAL FEATURE MAPS NACH M. HERRMANN / R. DER / G. BALZUWEIT

M. HERRMANN, R. DER und G. BALZUWEIT[100] beschreiben ein „Hierarchical Self-Organizing Maps for Non-Linear Component Analysis".

3.181 HIERARCHICAL SELF-ORGANIZING MAP NACH P. WEIERICH / M. v. ROSENBERG

P. WEIERICH und M. v. ROSENBERG[101] führen vor, wie temporale Strukturen und Kontexte von einem zweischichtigen SOM-Modell gelernt werden.

3.182 MULTILAYERED SELF-ORGANIZING FEATURE MAP (M-SOM) BZW. SCALEABLE SELF-ORGANIZING MAP (SSOM) NACH Hs. CHEN ET. ALT.

Der sgn."Multilayered Self-Organizing Feature Map (M-SOM)"- Algorithmus nach Hs. CHEN, Chr. SCHUFFELS und R. ORWIG[102] klassifiziert Internet Homepages basierend auf ihren Inhalten, und der sgn."Scaleable Self-Organizing Map (SSOM)"- Algorithmus von Hs. CHEN und Dm.G. ROUSSINOV[103] dient der Textklassifikation.

3.183 (NESTED) SOFTWARE SELF-ORGANIZING MAP ((N)SSOM) NACH H. YE / B.W.N. LO

Eine verbesserte Software Klassifikationstechnik bietet auch der „(Nested) Software Self-Organizing Map ((N)SSOM)"- Algorithmus von H. YE und B.W.N. LO[104].

3.184 MULTIPLE SELF-ORGANIZING FEATURE MAP NACH M. TAKATSUKA / R.A. JARVIS

Das sgn.„Multiple Self-Organizing Feature Map"- Modell von M. TAKATSUKA und R.A. JARVIS[105] beschreibt ein sgn.„3D Objects Encoding System" mit zwei SOMs mit hexagonaler Gitterstruktur, bestehend jeweils aus einer Standard SOM, zu der sgn.„reset neurons" und „buffer neurons" hinzugefügt werden, um globale Objekteigenschaften zu repräsentieren: die erste sgn. „Self-Organizing Feature Map for Surface Parts (SOFM_SP)" dient dabei der Analyse der Oberflächenteile und die zweite sgn.„Self-Organizing Feature Map for Geometrical Relationships (SOFM_GR)" dient der Kodierung der geometrischen Relationen zwischen Paaren von Oberflächenteilen.

3.2 TYPVARIANTE II.II: TREE-STRUCTURED SOMS

3.21 TREE-STRUCTURED TOPOLOGICAL FEATURE MAP (TSTFM) UND TREE-STRUCTURED SELF-ORGANIZING MAP (TS-SOM) NACH E. OJA / P. KOIKKALAINEN / J.T. LAAKSONEN / J.M. KOSKELA ET. ALT

Der sgn.„Tree-Structured Self-Organizing Map (TS-SOM)"- Algorithmus von E. OJA und P. KOIKKALAINEN[106] zeichnet sich durch eine hierarchische (Baum-) Pyramidenstruktur aus, wobei die Knoten des Baumes den Neuronen entsprechen und jede Baumebene oder -schicht einem einzelnen SOM-Netzwerk entspricht. Da jeweils nur eine Schicht trainiert wird, werden ihre Knoten „eingefroren" (engl.„frozen"), nachdem diese Schicht „organisiert" (engl.„organized") ist, und das Training wird mit der nächst tieferen Schicht fortgeführt. Die „eingefrorenen" Knoten stellen nun einen Suchbaum dar, der die Suche nach dem sgn.„best matching unit (BMU)" eingrenzt. Im Gegensatz zu den meisten Suchbaum-gestützten Algorithmen, bei denen zwei verschiedene (Vater-)Knoten nicht einen (Sohn-)Knoten teilen, kann man mit dem TS-SOM-Algorithmus i.V.m. dem sgn.„Probing Algorithm" die seitlichen SOM-Verbindungen dazu benutzen, festzustellen, ob die Nachbarknoten eine bessere Wahl für den BMU abgeben würden, was zur Folge hat, daß sich die Suchmengen von den Vater- zu den Sohnknoten „überlappen" (engl. „overlapping")[107] [108] [109]:

„In the following presentation *cur* is the currently adaptive layer, W_i is a weight vector, *Root* is the root node index, and *q* is the number of layers. First the weights of the root neuron are initialized to random values, and then the layers are trained sequentially.

> Initialize W_{root} = Random(); cur = 0;
> Organize The layers are trained sequentially
>   For all layers cur = 0,1, ..., q – 1
>   1. *Train-network-at(cur)*;
>   2. *Initialize(cur + 1)*;

The training procedure, *Train-network-at(cur)*, for the current layer, *cur*, is similar to the original SOM training. In the following presentation *Pick-ran-*

dom-from(·) is a random sampling function that selects one vector pattern, Ω is the set of training samples, *first* is the first (top) layer, $x(t)$ is the tth sample vector, and *BMU(cur)* is the best matching unit at the level *cur*. The convergence of the algorithm may vary from one application to another, in the simplest case it is limited to some number of iterations. Now the following steps are repeated until the network at level *cur* has converged.

1. Get sample $x(t) := $ *Pick-random-from(Ω)*;
2. Find BMU Call recursive function *Find BMU(·, ·, ·, ·)*, with parameters, $x(t)$, *cur*, *Root* and *first* to find the best matching unit BMU;
3. Update Update the weights of the BMU and its neighbors towards the given sample $x(t)$;
4. Repeat? $t := t + 1$; check convergence and adjust updating parameters;

The most important part of the TS-SOM algorithm is the search of the best matching unit (BMU). Search starts from the root node of the SOM structure and continues level by level until the best matching node from the currently adaptive layer *cur* is found. Whereas in normal tree search the search goes from the node to the best match of its sons, in TS-SOM search the next level BMU is selected from larger set of units: BMU is the best matching son of its fathers nearest neighbors (including the father). This algorithm is easily implemented via a recursive function that returns the BMU. As before, the search set is denoted by SN_c, and during the search variable *LAY* is the currently adaptive layer. Let us also denote $d(·, ·)$ as a function that returns a vector distance of its arguments, then the search algorithm is:

```
FUNCTION  Find-BMU( x(t), cur, BMU( LAY-1 ), LAY );
  IF ( LAY-1 = cur )  THEN
    BMU( cur ) := BMU( LAY-1 )
  ELSE  find BMU( LAY ) such that
```
$$\forall_k,\ k \in SN_{BMU(LAY-1)}:$$
$$d(W_{BMU(LAY)}, x(t)) \le d(W_k, x(t));$$
```
    and continue from the next tree level:
      BMU( cur ) := Find-BMU( x(t), cur, BMU( LAY ), LAY + 1 );
  ENDIF
  RETURN  BMU( cur )
END FUNCTION
```

Updating, *Update(x(t), BMU)*, is quite similar to any version of the SOM algorithm. (...) If N_c is the neighborhood of the neuron c, a is the adaptation constant ($0 < a << 1$) and t is the time discrete index, then one typical rule is:

$$W_k(t+1) := \begin{cases} W_k(t) + a\,[x(t) - W_k(t)], & \text{if } k \in N_{BMU} \\ W_k(t), & \text{otherwise} \end{cases}\text{."}[110]$$

Im Ergebnis reduziert der TS-SOM-Algorithmus die Trainingszeitkomplexität des Standard SOM-Algorithmus von $O(N)$ auf $O(log_pN)$, wobei N die Anzahl der Neuronen und p die Anzahl der Söhne des jeweiligen Baumknotens ist.

3.22 EVOLVING TREE NACH J. PAKKANEN / E. OJA ET. ALT.

Das sgn.„Evolving Tree"- Modell nach J. PAKKANEN, J. IIVARINEN und E. OJA [111] zeichnet sich – ebenso wie beim TS-SOM-Algorithmus – durch eine hierarchische (Baum-)Pyramidenstruktur aus, wobei jedoch – im Gegensatz zum TS-SOM-Algorithmus – der Wurzel- oder Stammknoten (engl.„root" oder „trunk node") und die Blätterknoten (engl.„leaf nodes") aus einzelnen Neuronen bestehen, die, sobald sie einen von vornherein festgelegten „Aufspaltungs-schwellenwert" (engl.„splitting threshold") überschritten haben, in eine vorher festgelegte Anzahl von neuen Knoten „aufgesplittet" werden. Die BMU-Suche gestaltet sich nun sehr ähnlich dem TS-SOM-Algorithmus, indem der Evolving Tree wie ein hierarchischer Suchbaum arbeitet. Um die Berechnung des Gitterdistanzwerts im Baum im Rahmen der Nachbarschaftsfunktion vornehmen zu können, wird der kürzeste Pfad vom BMU zum gewünschten Nachbarschaftsknoten anhand der Anzahl der Sprünge (engl.„hops") zwischen beiden minus eins berechnet, da nur die Distanz zwischen den Blätterknoten von Relevanz sein soll.

Das Evolving Tree-Modell[112] wird wie folgt beschrieben: „The Evolving Tree has nodes with prototype vectors, just like the SOM. Let us index the nodes by i and let $w_i \in IR^n$ denote the prototype or weight vector of node i. In addition to that, every node in the network has a counter b_i, giving the number of times it has been the best matching unit during training. (...)

The Evolving Tree algorithm starts by taking a single node and placing it at a suitable place in the data space. N obvious choice is the center of mass of the data cloud. Then we split the node. This means that we create a pre-determined amount of new nodes and mark them as the children of the split node. The weight vectors are initialized to that of the parent node, and for the next training vector, the BMU is randomly chosen among the children nodes in a manner described in the next chapter. In this way, the children weights separate from each other. We now have a tree structure with some amount of leaf nodes and one trunk node. All further manipulation operations are only done on the leaf nodes. Once created, a trunk node remains totally static, its only task is to maintain connections between other trunk and leaf nodes in the tree. Once a leaf node reaches a splitting threshold θ, having been the BMU for a given number of times, it is again split and so on. Thus a tree is formed recursively in the training algorithm.

Now we come to the novel parts of the algorithm: how to find the BMU in a tree and how to train the tree structure. To illustrate this process we now assume to have a larger tree structure (...). In this example every trunk node has two children. Finding the BMU is a top-down process. We start with a root node. Then we examine its children and find the node whose prototype vector is closest to the training vector. If that node is a leaf node, then it is the best matching unit. If not, its children are examined in turn and the closest one of them is chosen. This is repeated until a leaf node is found. Thus the Evolving Tree's trunk work as a hierarchical search tree for the leaf nodes. This method of finding the BMU is very similar to the one used in TS-SOM.

When the BMU has been determined, it is time to update the prototype vectors of the BMU, but also those of its neighbors, towards the training vector. The Evolving Tree uses the Kohonen learning rule to update node weight $w_i(t)$ towards the training vector $x(t)$ (...):

$$w_i(t+1)=w_i(t)+h_{ci}(t)[x(t)-w_i(t)]. \quad (1)$$

Here c is the index of the BMU and $h_{ci}(t)$ defines the neighborhood function. These are identical to their counterparts in the regular SOM algorithm. The counter b_c of the BMU is also incremented according to the following formula

$$b_c(t+1)=b_c(t)+1 \quad (2)$$

If we find after this incrementation that

$$b_c(t+1)=\theta \quad (3)$$

we split the BMU in the manner described above. This indicates that as the training continues, the tree keeps growing all the time. The speed of groth can be controlled by the θ parameter. If continuous growth is unwanted, it could be fixed by e.g. zeroing the counters between epochs. This is not currently implemented, because we have had no need for this functionality.
 A common choice for the neighborhood is the gaussian neighborhood

$$h_{ci}(t)=\alpha(t)\exp(\frac{\|r_c-r_i\|^2}{2\sigma^2(t)}). \quad (4)$$

The vectors r_c and r_i give the locations of nodes c and i on the SOM grid, the parameter $\alpha(t)$ defines the learning rate, and $\sigma(t)$ gives the width of the gaussian kernel.
 In the Evolving Tree parameters $\alpha(t)$ and $\sigma(t)$ work just like in the SOM. However, calculating the norm $\|r_c - r_i\|$ is not as simple. On the SOM it is just the grid distance between the node to be updated and the best matching unit. This is easy to calculate, because SOM is symmetric, static and has regular structure. None of these properties necessarily applies for the Evolving Tree.
 There is, however, a simple way to calculate an equivalent distance value in the tree. (...) In a tree structure, there is always the shortest path between any given two nodes. The minimal distances from the BMU node to all the other nodes in the tree can be computed using the following efficient algorithm. The basic idea is to calculate how many 'hops' must be done to get from the BMU to the desired node along this shortest path. The exact distance is the amount of hops minus one. One is subtracted because we are only interested in distances between leaf nodes. The closest possible leaf nodes have a common parent, so it takes two hops to get from one leaf to another. We want these 'closest neighbor' to have a distance of one, so we subtract one from all distances to retain consistency. (...)
 It should be noted that our choice of distance is unique and sensible. The way the Evolving Tree is formed ensures that there is one, and only one, path between any given leaf nodes (and also trunk nodes): Therefore the distance function is unique and symmetric. Since the path is unique, it must also

be the shortest path. These properties prove that the function is sensible mathematically. It is also suitable intuitively since we can assume that different branches of the tree grow to different areas of the data space. Therefore distances inside a branch are smaller than between different branches."

3.23 DYNAMIC SOM TREE NACH D. ALAHAKOON / S.K. HALGAMUGE / B. SRINIVASAN / A.L. HSU

D. ALAHAKOON, S.K. HALGAMUGE, B. SRINIVASAN und A.L. HSU[113] beschreiben eine Methode zur Konstruktion eines sgn.„Dynamic SOM Tree", bestehend aus neun Schichten von GSOMs (s. Kpt. 2.14) mit verschiedenen Werten des sgn.„spread factor" (s. Kpt. 2.14), die dazu dient „to achieve visualisation of cluster separation" und zur „automating cluster identification (...) to allow data analysts to aquire the desired number of clusters", und, unter Hinzuziehung des sgn.„Attribute-Custer Relationsship (ACR)"- Modells, „to enable rule generation of the automatically identified clusters" and to visualize „inter and intra cluster relationsships."

3.24 HIERARCHICAL FEATURE MAP (HFM) NACH R. MIIKKULAINEN

Das sgn.„Hierarchical Feature Map (HFM)"- System R. MIIKKULAINEN's[114] erkennt eine einzugebende Geschichte als eine Instanz eines partikulären „Skripts" i.S.v. R. SCHANK und R. ABELSON, indem es diese auf drei Ebenen klassifiziert in „scripts", „tracks" und in „role bindings", wobei die sich ergebende Neuronenstruktur sich als eine hierarchische Pyramide von Eigenschaftskarten darstellt, bei der zu jedem Neuron einer Karte in der darunterliegenden Ebene wieder eine neue Karte hinzugefügt wird, weshalb man m.E. diese Architektur zu den „Tree-Structured SOMs" zu zählen hat: „The higher-level map acts as a filter, (1) choosing the relevant items for each submap and (2) compressing the representation of these items to the most relevant components before passing them on for a more detailed mapping."[115]

3.25 HIERARCHICAL FEATURE MAP NACH D. MERKL

Basierend auf dem HFM-Modell R. MIIKKULAINEN's verwendet D. MERKL[116] dieses für die „text document classification task".

3.26 HIERARCHICAL SELF-ORGANISING NEURAL NETWORK NACH St.P. LUTTRELL

Das von St.P. LUTTRELL[117] verwendete sgn.„Hierarchical Self-Organising Neural Network" mit einer Binärbaumstruktur erzeugt ein hierarchisches Vektorquantisierungsschema, das die gesamte Vektorquantisierungsoperation bei hochdimensionalen Eingabedaten in eine Anzahl von Suboperationen mit niedriger Dimensionalität zerlegt, die nur einen geringen Berechnungsumfang erfordern. Diese Faktorisierung (engl.„factorisation") kann in der Bildverarbeitung und -kompression angewendet werden, indem – analog dem visuellen System beim Menschen – eine Vorverarbeitung (engl.„preprocessing") des

Bildes mit Hilfe von unüberwachten selbstorganisierenden neuronalen Net-
zen, z.B. dem SOM-Algorithmus stattfindet, gefolgt von einer Nachbearbei-
tung (engl.„post processing") des Bildes zum Zwecke seiner Klassifikation.

3.27 SPLITNET: TREE STRUCTURED NEURAL NETWORK NACH J. RAHMEL

Das sgn.„SplitNet"- Modell J. RAHMEL's[118] stellt ein dynamisch wachsendes
Baum-strukturiertes Netzwerk dar, das eine Hierarchie von ein-dimensionalen
KOHONEN-Ketten erzeugt, die in einer topologieerhaltenden Weise verbunden sind: „Topological defects in the chains are detected and resolved by
splitting a chain into linked parts (...). These subchains and the error minimizing insertion criterion for new neurons (...) (similar to the 'GCS-model B. FRITZ-
KE's' (A.d.V.)) provide the quantization properties of the network."

3.28 SELF-GENERATING NEURAL TREE (SGNT) NACH W.X. WEN / A. JENNINGS ET. ALT.

Das sgn.„Self-Generating Neural Tree (SGNT)"- Modell von W.X. WEN und A.
JENNINGS et. alt.[119] mit einer Baumstruktur-Topologie wird als eine Verbesse-
rung der Standard SOM vorgestellt.

3.291 HIERARCHICAL SELF-ORGANIZING MAP (HSOM) UND DYNAMIC AND HIERARCHICAL SELF-ORGANIZING MAP (DHSOM) NACH J.F.A. COSTA / M.L.A. NETTO ET. ALT.

In Anlehnung an R. MIIKKULAINEN's HFM und J. LAMPINEN's und E. OJA's
HSOM wird von J.F.A. COSTA / M.L.A. NETTO et. alt.[120] die Anwendung einer
„tree structured hierarchical SOM for image compression" präsentiert, die zu
einem sgn.„Hierarchical and Dynamic SOM (DHSOM)"- Modell weiterentwickelt wird.[121]

3.292 MULTILAYER KOHONEN FEATURE MAP NACH Kh.K. TRUONG ET. ALT.

Die Anwendung eines effizienten SOM-Algorithmus mit einer zweischichtigen Baumstruktur im Rahmen der sgn.„Bild-Codebook-Entwicklung" (engl.
„image codebook design") zeigen Kh.K. TRUONG und R.M. MERSETEAU.[122]

3.293 SELF-ORGANIZING TREE ALGORITHM (SOTA) NACH J. DOPAZO / J.M. CARA-ZO

Der sgn.„Self-Organizing Tree Algorithm (SOTA)" von J. DOPAZO / J.M. CA-
RAZO[123] besteht aus einer Binärbaum-Topologie unter der Verwendung von
B. FRITZKE's GCS-Algorithmus, die dazu dient, die genetischen Beziehungen
zwischen den Protein- oder Nukleotidsequenzen im Rahmen eines sgn.
„phylogentic tree" zu klassifizieren.

3.294 STRUCTURALLY ADAPTIVE INTELLIGENT NEURAL TREE (SAINT) NACH H.-H. SONG / S.-Wh. LEE

Das sgn.„Structurally Adaptive Intelligent Neural Tree (SAINT)"- Modell von H.-H. SONG und S.-Wh. LEE[124], führt eine hierarchische Partitionierung der Eingabemuster durch, indem ein Baum-strukturiertes Netzwerk, bestehend aus 2-dimensionalen Gitter-strukturierten Subnetzwerken, verwendet wird, wobei drei Operationen zur Strukturadaption vorgenommen werden können, u.z. indem Knoten erzeugt, entfernt oder miteinander verschmolzen werden können.

3.295 HIERARCHICAL SELF-ORGANIZING FEATURE MAP NACH Chr. KEMKE / A. WICHERT

Chr. KEMKE und A. WICHERT[125] verwenden in der Spracherkennung baumähnliche hierarchische KOHONEN-Karten, sgn.„hedges", wobei jeder Vaterknoten gemeinsame Kinder mit seinem Nachbarknoten haben kann.

4. ARCHITEKTURTYPVARIANTE III: GROWING HIERARCHICAL SOM VARIANTS

Sgn.„growing hierarchical self-organizing maps" verbinden die hierarchische Struktur der sgn.„multilayer self-organizing-maps" mit dem wachsenden Netzwerkverfahren der sgn.„growing self-organizing maps". Mit R.T. FREEMAN / H. YIN[126] gibt es zwei unterschiedliche Typen von sgn.„growing hierarchical SOM variants": Die eine Typvariante zeichnet sich dadurch aus, daß – z.B. in Analogie zum GG-Modell B. FRITZKE's oder zum IGG-Modell R. MIIKKULAINEN's und J. BLACKMORE's – eine rechteckige Gitterstruktur beibehalten wird (Typvariante III.I), wohingegen die andere von der GCS-Struktur B. FRITZKE's abgeleitet wird (Typvariante III.II).

4.1 TYPVARIANTE III.I: MAINTAINING A RECTANGULAR GRID

4.11 GROWING HIERARCHICAL SELF-ORGANIZING MAP (GHSOM) UND ADAPTIVE HIERARCHICAL INCREMENTAL GRID GROWING (AHIGG) NACH D. MERKL / M. DITTENBACH / A. RAUBER / M. KÖHLE ET. ALT.

Das sgn.„Growing Hierarchical Self-Organizing Map (GHSOM)"- Modell von D. MERKL, M.DITTENBACH, A. RAUBER et. alt.[127], sich gründend auf dem GG-Modell B. FRITZKE's und dem HFM-Modell R. MIIKKULAINEN's, setzt sich aus einer hierarchischen Struktur von mehreren sich nacheinander bildenden Schichten zusammen, wobei jede Schicht aus einer Anzahl von unabhängigen SOMs besteht, die ihre Netzform und -elemente während des Trainingsprozesses festlegen können und in denen für jedes Netzelement eine weitere SOM in der nächsten Schicht der Hierarchie hinzugefügt werden kann, weshalb sich dieses Modell bestens dazu eignet, mittels seiner adaptiven Architektur die hierarchischen Relationen in den einzugebenden Datenstrukturen zu repräsentieren: „We start with a 'virtual' layer 0, which consists of only one single unit. The weight vector of this unit is initialized as the average of all input data. The training process basically starts with a small map of, say, 2×2 units in layer 1, which is self-organized according to the standard SOM training algorithm. (...)
This training process is repeated for a fixed number λ of training iterations. Ever after λ training iterations the unit with the largest deviation between its weight vector and the input vectors represented by this very unit is selected as the error unit. In between the error unit and its most dissimilar neighbor in terms of the input space either a new row or a new column of units is inserted. The weight vectors of these new units are initialized as the average of their neighbors. This training process is highly similar to the Growing Grid model (...). The difference so far is that we use a decreasing learning rate and a decreasing neighborhood range instead of fixed values. Especially the fixed neighborhood range is problematic when the network grows to be larger after a series of insertions. (...)
An obvious criterion to guide the training process is the quantization error q_i. It is calculated as the sum of the distances between the weight vector of a unit i and the input vectors mapped onto this unit and may be used to evalu-

ate the mapping quality of a SOM based on the mean quantization error (MQE) of all units in the map. The lower the value of the MQE, the better the map is trained. A map grows until its MQE is reduced to a certain fraction T_1 of the q_i of the unit i in the preceding layer of the hierarchy. Thus, the map now represents the data mapped onto the higher layer unit i in more detail. (...)

As outlined above the initial architecture of the GH-SOM consists of one self-organizing map. This architecture is expanded by another layer in case of dissimilar input data being mapped on a particular unit. These units are identified by a rather high quantization error q_i which is above a threshold T_2. This treshold basically indicates the desired granularity level of data representation as a fraction of the initial quantization error at layer 0. In such a case, a new map will be added to the hierarchy and the input data mapped on the respective higher layer unit are self-organized in this new map, which again grows until its MQE is reduced to a fraction T_1 of the respective higher layer unit's quantization error q_i. Note that this may not necessarily lead to a balanced hierarchy. The depth of the hierarchy will rather reflect the ununiformity which should be expected in real-world data collections."[128][129]

Eine weiterentwickelte Version des GHSOM-Modells, das sgn.„Adaptive Hierarchical Incremental Grid Growing (AHIGG)"- Modell[130], gründet sich auf dem IGG-Konzept R. MIIKKULAINEN's und J. BLACKMORE's mit dem Hauptunterschied, verglichen mit dem GHSOM-Modell, daß „maps on individual layers may grow irregularly in shape and may remove connections between neighboring units."[131]

4.111 GROWING HIERARCHICAL SELF-ORGANIZING MAP (GHSOM) WITH THE TENSION AND MAPPING RATIO (TMR) NACH E. PAMPALK / G. WIDMER / A. CHAN

Mit der sgn.„Tension and Mapping Ratio"- Erweiterung versuchen nun E. PAMPALK, G. WIDMER und A. CHAN[132] die Unzulänglichkeiten des GHSOM-Algorithmus von D. MERKL, M.DITTENBACH, A. RAUBER et. alt. zu beheben: „The Tension and Mapping Ratio (TMR) extension of the basic GHSOM algorithm introduced here addresses in particular Decision 2A: Whether new units should be inserted and in which row or column they should be inserted. (...)

(...) the goal is to hierarchically cluster the data with clearly separated clusters on the top-layers and low quantization errors on the lower levels. (...)

The two principles of the TMR are straightforward. The first principle is to ensure stable mappings between two neighboring map units i and j. The stability is measured by inserting a virtual unit v_{ij} between the units i and j with its model vector $m_{ij} = (m_i + m_j)/2$. If a large number of items which are mapped to the units i and j would better be represented by v_{ij} then the arrangement is instable, on the other hand, if only a very small ratio of items would prefer v_{ij} then the relationsship is stable. We refer to this ratio as Mapping Ratio (MR).

The second principle is to ensure a stable structure of the neighborhood topology. The topology is stable if there is little Tension (T), i.e., if the distances between all neighbors are about the same. In particular, we calculate the Tension to avoid a disproportional ratio between the average pairwise distances between all adjacent rows and all adjacent columns."

4.12 HIERARCHICAL (OVERLAPPED) SELF-ORGANIZING MAP (HOSOM) NACH P.N. SUGANTHAN

Das sgn.„Hierarchical (Overlapped) Self-Organizing Map (HOSOM)"- Modell von P.N. SUGANTHAN[133] besitzt eine struktur-adaptive hierarchische Netzarchitektur mit ineinander übergreifenden hybriden Lernalgorithmen, die sowohl aus unüberwachten „SOM learning"- als auch aus überwachten „LVQ 2 learning"- Adaptionsphasen bestehen.

4.2 TYPVARIANTE III.II: DERIVED FROM THE GCS-STRUCTURE

4.21 HIERARCHICAL GROWING CELL STRUCTURES (TREEGCS) NACH V.J. HODGE / J. AUSTIN

Das sgn.„Hierarchical Growing Cell Structures (TreeGCS)"- Modell von V.J. HODGE und J. AUSTIN[134] ist auf dem GCS-Algorithmus B. FRITZKE's konstruiert und überlagert (engl.„superimpose") ihn: Der Baum besitzt jeweils einen Blattknoten, der für jeweils einen „GCS-Cluster" steht mit einer Liste aller Zellen der betreffenden Clusterzellstruktur und, sobald sich ein „Vaterknoten" (engl. „parent node") mit einem GCS-Cluster aufspaltet, wird die jeweilige Clusterzelliste zerstört und es werden neue „Kinderknoten" (engl.„child nodes") mit zum Baum hinzugefügt, um diese Spaltung wiederzuspiegeln, während ein Baumknoten entfernt wird, sobald der entsprechende GCS-Cluster entfernt worden ist. Alternativ können auch neu eingefügte Zellen einen neuen GCS-Cluster entstehen lassen: „(...) a new cluster may be formed from cells inserted during the current epoch so a new child node is added to the root and the cluster cells added to the new node's list."[135] Das Entfernen von Zellen erlaubt die Formation von Substrukturen, die einem Dendrogramm entsprechen, wobei jedoch, um die Stabilität der Zellstruktur sicherzustellen und zu verbessern, die Zellentfernungen erst dann durchgeführt werden, nachdem über 90% der maximalen Anzahl von Zellen erreicht ist: „A conceptual hierarchy of word synonym clusters is generated. The distance in the hierarchy between two concepts is inversely proportional to the similarity. Concepts are progressively more general and the cluster sets become larger towards the root of the hierarchy."[136] Den TreeGCS-Algorithmus hat man z.B. verwendet für die Organisation der „CIA World Factbooks".

4.22 GROWING AND SPLITTING NEURAL NETWORK NACH D. MERKL / M. KÖHLE

Ein sgn.„Growing and Splitting Neural Network"- Modell auf der Basis des GCS-Algorithmus B. FRITZKE's verwenden M. KÖHLE und D. MERKL[137] zur Klassifikation von Textdokumenten.

4.23 HIERARCHICAL GROWING CELL STRUCTURES (HiGS) NACH V. BURZEVSKI / Ch. K. MOHAN

Das sgn.„Hierarchical Growing Cell Structures (HiGS)"- Modell von V. BUR-ZEVSKI und Ch.K. MOHAN[138] stellt eine Baumnetzwerkstruktur dar, in welcher jedes Element aus einem GCS-Netzwerk B. FRITZKE's besteht.

4.3 TYPVARIANTE III.III: BASED ON A GROWING CHAIN (GC) ALGORITHM

4.31 ADAPTIVE TOPOLOGICAL TREE STRUCTURE (ATTS) NACH R.T. FREEMAN / H. YIN

Das sgn.„Adaptive Topological Tree Structure (ATTS)"- Modell von R.T. FREE-MAN und H. YIN[139] besteht aus einer (Baum-)Hierarchie aus 1-dimensionalen wachsenden SOM-Ketten (engl.„growing SOM chains"), deren Größe anhand eines Validierungsprozesses (engl.„validation process") unabhängig voneinander bestimmt wird, indem ein Entropie-basiertes BAYES'sches Informationskriterium (engl.„entropy-based Bayesian information criterion") verwendet wird.

4.4 TYPVARIANTE III.IV: BASED ON A BINARY TREE

4.41 DYNAMIC HIERARCHICAL SELF-ORGANIZING NEURAL NETWORKS NACH H.-L. HUNG / W.-Ch. LIN

Das sgn.„Dynamic Hierarchical Self-Organizing Neural Network"- Modell von H.-L. HUNG und W.-Ch. LIN[140] besteht aus einer Binärbaum-Topologie, dessen Neuronen dynamisch erzeugt werden, und die Anpassung der Gewichtsvektoren anhand der sgn.„fuzzy covariance matrix procedure" vorgenommen wird, sodaß zu einem bestimmten Anpassungszeitpunkt alle Eingabedaten gleichzeitig herangezogen werden.

5. ARCHITEKTURTYPVARIANTE IV: ADAPTIVE SUBSPACE SELF-ORGANIZING MAP (ASSOM) NACH T. KOHONEN ET. ALT.

5.1 ADAPTIVE SUBSPACE SELF-ORGANIZING MAP (ASSOM) NACH T. KOHONEN ET. ALT.

Die sgn.„Adaptive Subspace Self-Organizing Map (ASSOM)" von T. KOHONEN et. alt.[141] besteht – im Gegensatz zur „Basic SOM" – nicht aus einem Neuron mit einem zugehörigen Gewichtsvektor, sondern aus einem regelmäßigen Array von „neuralen" Modulen, wobei jedes Modul einen linearen, von adaptiven Basisvektoren aufgespannten Unter(-vektor-)raum (engl.„subspace") $L^{(i)}$ des Eingaberaums repräsentiert derart, daß jedes Modul eine orthogonale Projektion einer „Episode" (engl.„episode") S von Eingabedaten, d.h. einer Serie von demselben Unterraum angehörenden Datenvektoren, in seinen linearen Unterraum durchführt. Nachdem ein Gewinnerunterraum (engl.„winner subspace") $L^{(c)}$ bestimmt wird, indem das Modul ausgewählt wird, das die größte Energie in den orthogonalen Projektionen der Datenvektoren in seinen Unterraum hat, was gleichbedeutend ist mit der Auswahl des Moduls mit der minimalsten Summe des Restfehlers (engl.„residual error"), und sofern dieses Modul der richtigen Klasse der Daten entspricht, werden die Basisvektoren des Unterraums gemäß der sgn.„Learning Subspace Method (LSM)" einer Rotation unterworfen derart, daß sich die sgn.„Projektionsenergie" (engl.„projection energy") der Datenvektoren erhöht, sodaß nach der Selbstorganisation benachbarte Module ähnlich orientierte Unterräume besitzen. Der ASSOM-Algorithmus ist damit in der Lage – bis zu einem bestimmten Grad – die invarianten Eigenschaften von Mustern zu gewinnen, wenn sie verschiedenen Transformationen ausgesetzt worden sind, wie z.B. Translationen, Rotation und Skalierung, m.a.W., es ist gezeigt worden, daß der ASSOM-Algorithmus die Fähigkeit besitzt, sgn.„wavelet filters" zu extrahieren, wie z.B. den sgn.„GABOR-Filter", in Antwort auf zufällige Bildsignale, die geringen Transformationen unterzogen worden waren sowie in bezug auf Sprachsignale.

Das ASSOM-Modell wird von T. KOHONEN selbst wie folgt beschrieben: „We shall show below that there exists a special kind of SOM, called the Adaptive-Subspace SOM (ASSOM), in which the various map units adaptively develop into filters of many basic invariant features. The mathematical forms of these filters need not be fixed a priori; the filters and their mixture find their forms automatically in response to typical transformations that occur in observations. (...)

If, instead of referring to weight vectors of neurons as templates for patterns, a 'neural' unit of the SOM is made to represent a manifold such as a linear subspace, the SOM units will then be able to match certain elementary patterns under some of their basic transformations such as translation, rotation, and scaling.

Let us recall (...) that a linear subspace is a manifold, defined as the general linear combination of its basic vectors. We shall show below that a new kind of SOM, the ASSOM, can be constructed of neural units that represent linear subspaces, and invariant feature detectors for various wavelets will emerge at the map units during learning. (...)

If the basis vectors of the subspaces are chosen in a suitable way, for instance, as certain kinds of elementary patterns (representations of features), the different linear subspaces can be made to represent different invariance groups of these elementary patterns. As already mentioned, we shall further show that the basis vectors can be learned completely automatically, without assumption of any mathematical forms for them, in response to pieces of sequences of input signals that contain these transformations. In the ASSOM, every map unit is made to represent its own subspace with a small dimensionality, say, two, and the basis vectors are determined adaptively, following the idea of the Adaptive-Subspace Theorem (...). The fundamental difference with respect to the latter is that we now have many subspaces instead of one that compete on the same input; the 'winner subspace' and its neighbors will learn the present sequence, whereas other sequences may be learned by other 'winners' at other times.

As emphasized before, another fundamental difference between the basic SOM and the ASSOM algorithm is thus that a map unit is not described by a single weight vector, but the unit is supposed to represent a linear subspace spanned by the adaptive basic vectors. Matching thereby does not mean comparison of dot products or Euclidean differences of the input and weight vectors, but comparison of orthogonal projections of the input vector on the different subspaces represented by the different map units. Accordingly, the learning step must modify all the basis vectors that define the selected subspaces.

The most essential function in the ASSOM, however, is competitive learning of episodes, whereupon it is not a pattern but a sequence of patterns on which the map units compete, and to which they are adapting. This scheme does not occur in any other neural-network model.

The ASSOM algorithm may also be thought to differ from all the other neural-network algorithms in the respect that it does not learn particular patterns, but rather transformation kernels."[142]

„Let us recall that the purpose of the ASSOM is to learn a number of various invariant features, usually pieces of elementary one- or two-dimensional waveforms with different frequencies called the 'wavelets', independent of their phase. These waveforms will be represented and analyzed by special filters, resembling the Gabor filters, and phase-invariant filtering is usually implemented by summing up the squares of the outputs of two associated orthogonal linear filters. This pair of linear filters carries out convolution-type integral transforms, and the kernels of the transformation pair constitute matched filters to the 'wavelets', one of them usually corresponding to the cosine transform, and the other to the sine transform, respectively. In principle it is also possible to use more than two orthogonal filters to describe a wavelet, but for simplicity we shall restrict to filter pairs in this discussion.

The formalism used to implement these filters adaptively is that of the learning-subspace classifier (...). The basis vectors of the subspaces will be learned from input data and they then correspond to the transformation kernels; since we are mainly interested in the cosine- and sine-type transformation, the number of orthogonal basis vectors in all the subspace classifiers discussed in this section will also be restricted to two.

 The subspaces that represent these filters are associated with the neural units of a special SOM architecture, they are made to compete on the same inputs during learning; in this way they learn how they shall mutually partition the input signal space. The Adaptive-Subspace (AS) Theorem (...) already described how a single 'neural' subspace can be made to converge to a subspace spanned by a small number of adjacent input signal samples, i.e., to become a subset of the latter. If there are several 'neural' subspaces, they will thus competitively partition the signal space into a number of subspaces, each one describing its own signal manifold (wavelet set)."[143]

„An essential new idea we need in the sequel is the concept of a 'representative winner' for a set of subsequent sequences, i.e., a set of $x(t)$ vectors that occur adjacent in time. In a traditional SOM we can, of course, define the usual 'winner' node $c = c(t)$ for every $x(t)$, but what we actually want a particular map unit and its neighborhood in the ASSOM array to do is to learn the general linear combination of adjacent sequences $x(t)$. If a particular neural unit has to become sensitive to a whole set of temporally adjacent sequences independently of their phases (or shift in the time scale), i.e., to a subset of input vectors, then obviously the 'winner' must be defined for that whole subset of temporally adjacent sequences of samples, which we shall call the episode. The winner shall be fixed for the whole episode during a learning step. All the adjacent $x(t)$ will then be learned by he 'representative winner' unit and its neighboring units in the array during the step.

 It may help to understand this idea if we consider that during a short episode S, equivalent with a set of successive sampling instants $\{t_p\}$, we have collected a set of input vectors $\{x(t_p)\}$, each member of which represents a sample of a sequence and all these sequences are linearly dependent. (There may also exist other, linearly independent components in the input, but they will be regarded as noise and smoothed out in the learning process.) In particular, if S is finite and eventually rather small, the $\{x(t_p)\}$ during it may be thought to span a signal subspace X of a much lower dimensionality than n. Consider also a set of operational units that will be identified with the SOM (ASSOM) units a little later. With each unit we can associate its own subspace $L^{(i)}$. If we then identify the 'winner' subspace $L^{(c)}$ to which X is closest, $L^{(c)}$ may be regarded to approximate X better than any other $L^{(i)}$.

 The main problem in matching signal subspaces X with the 'neural' subspaces $L^{(i)}$ is that since the number of samples in the episodes S can be taken as arbitrary, the dimensionality of the subspaces X spanned by the $x(t_p)$ becomes arbitrarily defined, too. Therefore this author has suggested a simpler and more robust method for the matching of an episode with the 'neural' subspaces. Consider the 'energy of the projections' of the $x(t_p)$, $t_p \in S$, on the different $L^{(i)}$. This 'energy' is defined as the sum of squared projections over the episode on each of the $L^{(i)}$. Then the maximum of these entities shall define the 'representative winner' (over the episode), denoted by c_r: (...)

 This 'representative winner' is fixed for the whole S, and the units at or around index c are made to learn X as described by the Adaptive-Subspace Theorem

(...)."[144]

„The Self-Organizing Map (SOM) is in general a regular (...) array of neural cells (...). The Adaptive-Subspace SOM (ASSOM) also relates to an array of 'neural' units, but each unit in it describes a subspace. Such a unit may be composed physically of several neurons (...). Following the subspace classifier principle, the ASSOM algorithm is defined in detail as"[145]:

1. Locate the unit, the „representative winner", indexed by c_r and on which the „projection energy" is maximum:

$$c_r = \arg\max_i \left\{ \sum_{t_p \in S} \|\hat{x}^{(i)}(t_p)\|^2 \right\}.$$

2. For each sample vector $x(t_p)$ of the episode S:

2.1 Rotate the basis vectors $b_h{}^{(i)}$ of the winner unit and units in its neighborhood in the neural-unit array:

$$b_h'^{(i)} = b_h^{(i)}(t+1) = \prod_{t_p \in S} \left[I + \alpha(t_p) \frac{x(t_p) x^T(t_p)}{\|\hat{x}^{(i)}(t_p)\| \, \|x(t_p)\|} \right] b_h^{(i)}(t_p).$$

Using $h_{cr\,i}$ to denote the neighborhood interactions, the learning law was:

$$b_h'^{(i)} = b_h^{(i)}(t+1) = \prod_{t_p \in S} \left[I + \alpha(t_p) h_{c_r i} \frac{x(t_p) x^T(t_p)}{\|\hat{x}^{(i)}(t_p)\| \, \|x(t_p)\|} \right] b_h^{(i)}(t_p),$$

in which the basis vectors are formed by a product of elementary projection operators, each one corresponding to one pattern $x(t_p)$, $t_p \in S$. The special learning-rate factor $\lambda = \alpha(t_p) \dfrac{\|(t_p)\|}{\|\hat{x}^{(i)}(t_p)\|}$ has been chosen for stability reasons. This „rotation" must be restricted to the units $i \in N^{(cr)}$, where $N^{(cr)}$ is the neighborhood of the „representative winner" in the ASSOM network.

This defines the basis vectors $b_h{}^{(i)}$ and a set of analyzers that are optimally invariant to the transformations that occur in the input signal patterns.

2.2 Dissipate the components $b_{hj}{}^{(i)}$ of the basis vectors $b_h{}^{(i)}$:

$$b_{hj}'^{(i)} = \mathrm{sgn}(b_{hj}^{(i)}) \max(0, |b_{hj}^{(i)}| - \epsilon), \text{ where}$$

$$\epsilon = \epsilon_h^{(i)}(t) = \delta |b_h^{(i)}(t) - b_h^{(i)}(t-1)|.$$

2.3 Orthonormalize the basis vectors $b_h{}^{(i)}$ of each winner unit and units in its neighborhood in the neural-unit array.[146] [147]

5.2 ADAPTIVE SUBSPACE SELF-ORGANIZING MAP (ASSOM) NACH H.-U. BAUER ET. ALT.

Ein der „Adaptive Subspace SOM" ähnliches Modell, vorgestellt von H.-U. BAU-ER et. alt.[148], bei der der Algorithmus in seinen formalen Bedingungen „gelok-kert" worden war, um eine plausiblere neurale Implementation zu erreichen, erlaubt die Erhärtung von Belegen für die fehlende Repräsentation der Phasen im visuellen Kortex von Säugetieren.

5.3 ADAPTIVE MANIFOLD SELF-ORGANIZING MAP (AMSOM) NACH Zh.-Q. LIU

Das sgn.„Adaptive Manifold Self-Organizing Map (AMSOM)"- Modell von Zh.-Q. LIU[149] modifiziert die „Standard ASSOM" insofern, daß, auf der Basis einer 2-dimensionalen hexagonalen Architektur in den Modulen, anstelle von Unterräumen Mannigfaltigkeiten (engl.„manifolds") anhand des mittleren Vektors (engl.„mean vector") gelernt werden und wendet dies im Bereich der Gesichtserkennung an.

5.4 ADAPTIVE SUBSPACE SELF-ORGANIZING MAP (ASSOM) NACH B. ZHANG ET. ALT.

Eine Anwendung des ASSOM-Modells als ein modulares Klassifikationsschema in bezug auf handgeschriebene Buchstabenerkennung wird von B. ZHANG et. alt.[150] vorgestellt.

6. ARCHITEKTURTYPVARIANTE V: ALTERNATIVE SOM VARIANTS

6.1 SOM WITH CALCULATED FRACTAL DIMENSION NACH H. SPECKMANN / G. RAD-DATZ / W. ROSENSTIEL

Zum Zwecke einer korrekten Topologieerhaltung und der verbesserten Analyse der Kartenentwicklung während der Lernphase ist von H. SPECKMANN, G. RAD-DATZ und W. ROSENSTIEL[151] die Methode der fraktalen geometrischen Dimensionsberechnung einer SOM entwickelt worden, wobei, basierend auf der Berechnung einer Attraktordimension in der Theorie der nicht-linearen dynamischen Systeme, die fraktale (Informations-)Dimension eines gegebenen Datensatzes bestimmt wird und einer selbstorganisierenden Karte als deren fraktale geometrische Dimension zugewiesen wird.

6.2 HYPERBOLIC, TOROIDAL, SPHERICAL UND CIRCULAR SOM VARIANTS

6.21 HYPERBOLIC SELF-ORGANIZING MAP (HSOM) UND HIERARCHICALLY GROWING HYPERBOLIC SELF-ORGANIZING MAP (H²SOM) NACH H. RITTER / J. ONTRUP

Das sgn.„Hyperbolic Self-Organizing Map (HSOM)"- Modell von H. RITTER und J. ONTRUP[152] mit Anwendungen im Bereich „text categorization", „semantic browsing" und „semantic navigation"[153] und mit einer Erweiterung zum sgn. „Hierarchically Growing Hyperbolic Self-Organizing Map (H²SOM)"[154] zeichnet sich dadurch aus, daß bei sehr komplexen hierarchischen Informationsstrukturen mehr Nachbarschaftsbeziehungen in die räumliche Umgebung einer Karteneinheit passen, da im Rahmen einer RIEMANN'schen hyperbolischen Geometrie unter Verwendung der sgn.„Hyperbolischen Fläche H2" die Größe der Nachbarschaft um einen Punkt exponentiell mit dem Radius r wächst. Beim HSOM-Modell wird nun – als ein Äquivalent für ein regelmäßiges Gitter in der hyperbolischen Ebene – eine regelmäßige Dreieckstesselierung mit Vertexordnung sieben vorgenommen, sodaß sich die Knoten eines solchen Gitters wie „Ringe" um einen Ursprungsknoten anordnen. Da es aber keine isometrische, d.h. distanzerhaltende, Einbettung einer hyperbolischen Fläche in einen euklidischen Raum gibt, verwendet man stattdessen eine isometrische Einbettung in einen 3-dimensionalen Raum mit einer nichteuklidischen MINKOWSKI Pseudometrik, von der aus das sgn.„KLEIN-Modell" und das sgn. „POINCARÉ-Modell" konstruiert werden, wobei letzteres zur Veranschaulichung des HSOM-Modells dient, das dann in der gewohnten Weise trainiert wird, indem der Gewinnerknoten s bestimmt wird, und danach alle Knoten r in einer radialen Gitternachbarschaft N um s angepaßt werden.
Das HSOM-Modell wird von H. RITTER wie folgt beschrieben: „While the sphere is characterized by a constant positive gaussian curvature (i.e., the surface 'bends' into the same perpendicular direction, as one moves along two orthogonal directions), there are also surfaces that possess negative gaussian curvature. The counterpart of the sphere is achieved by requiring a constant negative curvature everywhere, and the resulting space is known

as the hyperbolic plane H2 (...). Unfortunately, it is no longer possible to embed H2 in a (distance-preserving) way in our euclidean IR³, but we still can do so with sufficiently small 'patches' of H2. The embedded patches then resemble the shape of a 'saddle', i.e., the negative curvature shows up as a local bending into opposite normal directions, as we move on orthogonal lines along the patch. This may make it intuitively plausible that on such surfaces the area (and also the circumference) of a circular neighborhood around a point now grows faster than in the uncurved case. The geometry of H2 is a standard topic in Riemannian geometry (...), and the relationships for the area A and the circumference C of a circle of radius r are given by

$$A = 4\pi \sinh^2(r/2) \quad (1)$$
$$C = 2\pi \sinh(r) \quad (2)$$

These formulae exhibit the highly remarkable property that both quantities grow exponentially with the radius r (...). It is the property (...) to make hyperbolic spaces extremely useful for accommodating hierarchical structures: their neighborhoods are in a sense 'much larger' than in the non-curved euclidean (or in the even 'smaller' positively curved) spaces (it makes also intuitively understanable why no finite-dimensional euclidean space allows an (isometric) embedding: it only has space for a power-law-growth).

To use this potential for the SOM, we must solve two problems: (*i*) we must find suitable discretization lattices on H2 to which we can 'attach' the SOM prototyp vectors. (*ii*) after having constructed the SOM, we must somehow project the (hyperbolic!) lattice into 'flat space' in order to be able to inspect the generated maps (...). (...)

While the structure of hyperbolic spaces makes it impossible to find an isometric (ie., distance-preserving) embedding into a euclidean space, there are several ways to construct very useful embeddings under weaker conditions (...). The closest analogy to the sphere-embedding occurs if we sacrifice the euclidean structure of the embedding space and instead endow it with a Minkowski-metric (...). (...)

From this embedding, we can construct two further ones, the so-called Klein model and the Poincaré model (the latter will be used to visualize hyperbolic SOMs below). (...)

To complete the set-up for a hyperbolic SOM we still need an equivalent of a regular grid in the hyperbolic plane. Fortunately, the tesselation of hyperbolic spaces is a well developed subject in the mathematics literature (...). (...)

One way to generate these tesselations algorithmically is by repeated application of a suitable set of generators of their symmetry group to a (suitably sized, cf. below) 'starting triangle'. (...)

In a hyperbolic space, specifying the angles of a triangle automatically fixes its size: unlike the euclidean case, the angles no longer sum up to π, instead, the sum is always less and the 'deficit' equals the area of the triangle. Therefore, the smallest triangles are obtained for the minimal value of $n = 7$, which, therefore, leads to the 'finest' tesselation and will be our choice for the simulations reported below. Since the resulting lattice structure is very different from a rectangular array, there is no straightforward indexing scheme and

an efficient implementation has to store pointers to the topological neighbors of each newly generated vertex in order to allow iterating the SOM update step over the lattice neighborhood of each winner node. (...)
We have now all ingredients required for a 'hyperbolic SOM'. It employs a (finite patch) of a hyperbolic lattice, e.g., the regular triangle tesselation with vertex order $n = 7$. Using the construction scheme sketched in the previous section, we can organize the nodes of such a lattice as 'rings' around an origin node (ie., it is simplest to build approximately 'circular' latices). The numbers of nodes of such a lattice grows very rapidly (asymptotically exponentially) with the chosen lattice radius R (its number of rings). (...) Each lattice node r carries a prototyp vector

$$\vec{w}_r \in IR^D$$

from some D-dimensional feature space (...). The SOM is then formed in the usual way, e.g., in on-line mode by repeatedly determining the winner node s and adjusting all nodes $r \in N(s,t)$ in a radial lattice neighborhood $N(s,t)$ around s according to the familiar rule

$$\Delta \vec{w}_r = \eta\, h_{rs}(\vec{x} - \vec{w}_r) \qquad (9)$$

with $h_{rs} = \exp(-d^2(r,s)/2\sigma^2)$. However, since we now work on a hyperbolic lattice, we have to determine both the neighborhood $N(s,t)$ and the (squared) node distance $d^2(r,s)$ according to the natural metric that is inherited by the hyperbolic lattice.
The simplest way to do this is to keep with each node r a complex number z_r to identify its position in the hyperbolic space (it is convenient to use the Poincaré model (...). The node distance is then given (...) as

$$d = 2\,\mathrm{arctanh}\left(\left|\frac{z_r - z_s}{1 - \bar{z}_s \cdot z_r}\right|\right) \qquad (10)$$

The neighborhood $N(t, s)$ can be defined as the subset of nodes within a certain graph distance (which is chosen as a small multiple of the neighborhood radius σ) around s. In our current implementation, we use a recursive node traversal scheme which is more costly than a scheme optimized for a particular lattice type; however, it still is reasonably fast and has the virtue that it can be used for arbitrary latice topologies."[155]

6.22 TORUS SOM NACH M. ITO / Ts. MIYOSHI / H. MASUYAMA

Eine sgn.„Torus SOM" nach M. ITO, Ts. MIYOSHI und H. MASUYAMA[156] wird vorgestellt, ohne daß jedoch näher auf die Netzstruktur eingegangen wird.

6.23 TOROIDAL SELF-ORGANIZING FEATURE MAP (TSOFM) NACH G. ANDREU / A. CRESPO / J.M. VALIENTE

Um den sgn.„border effect" (s. Kpt. 7.1) in einem Netzwerk zu reduzieren, wird mit dem sgn.„Toroidal Self-Organizing Feature Map (TSOFM)"- Modell von G. ANDREU, A. CRESPO und J.M. VALIENTE[157] eine neue Definition der topologischen Distanz und der topologischen Nachbarschaft eingeführt.

6.24 SPHERICAL SELF-ORGANIZING FEATURE MAP (SOFM) NACH G.K. KNOPF / A. SANGOLE

Im sgn.„Spherical Self-Organizing Feature Map (SOFM)"- Modell von G.K. KNOPF und A. SANGOLE[158] besteht das Einheitsgitter aus einer „Mosaik"-Einheitssphäre (engl.„tesselated unit sphere") mit einheitlichen Dreieckselementen, wobei jeder Knoten auf der tesselierten Sphäre eine Clustereinheit (engl. „cluster unit") darstellt: „Each input vector is connected to every cluster unit in the spherical network by a weight vector $w_{i,j,k}$. (...) Every cluster unit located at (i,j,k) has a neighborhood ($NE_{i,j,k}$) of one unit radius associated with it."[159]

6.25 ANGULAR QUANTISING SELF ORGANISING MAP NACH St. McGLINCHEY / C. FYFE

Das sgn.„Angular Quantising Self Organising Map"- Modell von ST. McGLINCHEY / C. FYFE[160] besteht aus einer 2-dimensionalen Karte, die um eine 3-dimensionale Sphäre konvergieren soll, d.h. jede ihrer Reihen von Neuronen stellt eine horizontale Schicht (engl.„slice") der Sphäre dar, wobei der Breitenwinkel (engl.„angle of latitude") zwischen benachbarten Scheiben gleich sein soll.

6.26 CIRCULAR KOHONEN NETWORK NACH V.-E. NEAGOE

Zur „image vector quantization" verwendet V.-E. NEAGOE[161] zwei sgn.„circular Kohonen networks" mit 256 bzw. 1024 Neuronen, ohne auf die Netzstruktur näher einzugehen.

6.27 CIRCULAR/WRAP-AROUND SELF-ORGANIZING MAP NETWORK NACH M.Y. KIANG / U.R. KULKARNI ET. ALT.

Im sgn.„Circular/Wrap-around Self-Organizing Map Network" versuchen M.Y. KIANG und U.R. KULKARNI et. alt.[162], den sgn.„boundary effect" (s. Kpt. 7.1) dadurch zu umgehen, daß eine kontinuierliche 2-dimensionale Kohonen-Schicht erzeugt wird, indem mit dem sgn.„circular weight-adjustment algorithm" die Reihen und Spalten „rundherum" (engl.„wrap around") um eine quadratische Kohonen-Schicht rotiert werden, sodaß, da nur die relative Stelle der Referenzvektoren auf der Karte relevant ist, die Nachbarschaft auch auf die entgegengesetzte Ecke der Schicht ausgeweitet wird.

6.3 (HIERARCHICAL) PARAMETRIZED SELF-ORGANIZING MAP (PSOM) NACH H. RITTER / J. WALTER ET. ALT.

Mit dem sgn.„Parametrized Self-Organizing Map (PSOM)"- Modell H. RITTER's und J. WALTER's et. alt.[163] erhält man eine kontinuierliche, parametrisierte (engl. „parametrized") Repräsentation der Eingabedaten in den Ausgaberaum, wobei die Mannigfaltigkeit der Karte (engl.„map manifold") aufgespannt wird an-

hand einer kleinen Menge von sgn.„Basis- oder Prototypmannigfaltigkeiten"
(engl.„basis or prototype manifolds"), weshalb dies nur sehr wenige Referenzvektoren für die Konstruktion der PSOM-Karte erfordert, m.a.W. die Referenzvektoren repräsentieren die Karte nicht mehr direkt, stattdessen wird die „lokale" (engl.„localist") Repräsentation durch ein mehr verteiltes Schema (engl.
„distributed scheme") ersetzt, in dem die parametrisierte Karte von einer Menge von Basismannigfaltigkeiten aufgebaut wird, wobei der Beitrag jeder Basis-
mannigfaltigkeit von einem der Referenzvektoren gesteuert wird, so daß „glatte Kartierungen" (engl.„smooth mappings") von nur sehr wenigen Datenstich-
proben erzeugt werden können: „Each point on a d-dimensional self-organizing map can be identified by a d-tuple s of 'map coordinates' $s = (s_1, s_2 ... s_d)$. In
the case of a standard SOM the allowed values of s are restricted to a discrete
set $\tilde{A}$ of lattice points, and each lattice point s is assigned a reference vector
$w_s \in V$ of the data ('feature') space V. Geometrically, this can be thought of as
an embedding of the discrete lattice $\tilde{A}$ in V. Each point $x \in V$ is then mapped
to a lattice point $s(x) \in \tilde{A}$ by minimizing the distance $d(x, w_s) = \|x - w_s\|$, consid-
ered as a function of s.

A parametrized self-organizing map generalizes this scheme to a manifold A
on which the map coordinates s may vary continuously. As a consequence,
the discrete assignment of reference vectors w_s is replaced by a continuous,
vector-valued function $w : A \rightarrow V, s \rightarrow w(s) \in V$, and the map image $s(x)$ of a
point $x \in V$ is found by minimizing the distance $d(x, w(s)) = \|x - w(s)\|$ with re-
spect to the now continuous variable s (see below).

Since we want to construct a PSOM from an associated, discrete SOM with
lattice $\tilde{A}$, we will require that $w(s) = w_s$ on the set $\tilde{A} \subset A$ of lattice locations of
the underlying SOM. For all intermediate positions s, $w(s)$ shall interpolate
smoothly between these values. These conditions will not specify $w(\cdot)$ uniquely,
but a convenient, sufficiently general form results with the ansatz

$$w(s)= \sum_{a \in \tilde{A}} H(s,a)w_s. \quad (1)$$

Here, $H(s, a)$ is a family of basis functions, one for each lattice location $a \in \tilde{A}$,
that must meet the orthogonality requirement

$$H(a,a')=\delta_a,a' \quad \forall a,a' \in \tilde{A} \quad (2)$$

on the subset of lattice locations $\tilde{A}$. This will guarantee the property $w(s) = w_s$
on $\tilde{A}$. (...)

Geometrically, equation 1 can be interpreted as a construction of the map
manifold A from a discrete family of 'basis manifolds' given by the function
$H(s,a)$. (...)

To determine the image $s(x)$ of an input vector x in the PSOM requires minimization of the distance $d(x, w(s))$. An explicit solution of this minimization task is
not possible in general. Instead, one has to resort to an iterative procedure.
The simplest approach is to use gradient descent in the variables s, with the
value s^* obtained from a prior best-match search on the discrete lattice $\tilde{A}$ as a
starting value $s(t = 0)$. Successive approximations $s(t)$ to the minimizing $s(x)$ can
then be obtained from

$$s(t+1)=s(t)+\gamma(t)J(s)^{T}P(x-w(s(t)))\qquad(3)$$

Here, $\gamma(t) > 0$ is a step size parameter, $J(s)$ is the Jacobian $\partial w(s) / \partial s$ evaluated at the current point, and P is an (optional) projection matrix (see below). Equation 3 can be viewed as a network dynamics for a recurrent network, however, with node activities represented parametrically by the map coordinate vector s. (...)
A final note concerns the possibility to adapt a PSOM as additional data vectors x become available. Stochastic gradient descent for the reference vectors w_s yields the adaptation rule

$$\Delta w_{a}=\epsilon H(s,a)(x-w_{a}),\qquad\forall a\in\tilde{A}\qquad(4)$$

where ϵ is a learning rate parameter and $s = s(x)$ is the map location computed from the network dynamics equation 3 in response to an input x. Equation 4 is the PSOM-equivalent for the Kohonen adaptation rule, however, with the role of the neighborhood function now taken by the basis functions $H(s, a)$, which, in general, will vary with the lattice site a."[164]
„The PSOM concept (...) can be seen as the generalization of the SOM with the following three main extensions:
· The index space S in the Kohonen map is generalized to a continuous mapping manifold $S \in \mathbb{R}^m$.
· The embedding space $X = X^{in} \times X^{out} \subset \mathbb{R}^d$ is formed by the Cartesian product of the input space and output space.
· We define a continuous mapping $w(\cdot)$: $s \to w(s) \in M \subset X$, where s varies continuously over $S \subseteq \mathbb{R}^m$. "[165]

6.4 BACK-PROPAGATION (BP)-SOM ARCHITECTURE NACH T. WEIJTERS / A. van den BOSCH / H. JAAP van den HERIK ET. ALT.

Die sgn.„Back-Propagation (BP)-SOM Architecture" nach T. WEIJTERS, A. van den BOSCH und H. JAAP van den HERIK et. alt.[166] kombiniert die traditionelle sgn.„backpropagation learning rule" (dt.„Fehlerrückrechnungslernregel") eines sgn.„multilayer feedforward network (MFN)" mit dem unüberwachten Lernen des SOM-Algorithmus, u.z. je eine SOM für jede versteckte Schicht (engl. „hidden layer") des MFN: „While the MFN is trained, the accompanying SOMs are also trained with the hidden-unit activations of the MFN. Relative to a certain level of self-organization in the SOMs, information from the SOMs is used during the updating of the connection weights of the MFN as input vectors. The effect is that hidden-unit activations of patterns that associated with the same clas, will tend to become more similar to each other."[167]

6.5 DOUBLE SELF-ORGANIZING FEATURE MAP (DSOM) NACH M.-Ch. SU / H.-T. CHANG

Das sgn.„Double Self-Organizing Feature Map (DSOM)"- Modell von M.-Ch. SU und H.-T. CHANG[168] besteht aus einer 2-dimensionalen rechteckigen Gitterstruktur, in der nicht nur die Synapsenvektoren der Neuronen angepaßt wer den, sondern auch deren 2-dimensionale Positionsvektoren (engl.„plane vectors") im Rahmen einer nicht-linearen Projektion in einen kontinuierlichen Ausgaberaum.

7. KRITIK UND EVALUATION

7.1 KRITIK AN DER STANDARD SOM T. KOHONEN'S

Das Standard SOM-Modell von T. KOHONEN ist nun in der Literatur[169] aufgrund von gewissen Problemen im praktischen Einsatz kritisiert worden, was u.a. auch den Bereich der Netzwerktopologie, d.h. der Netzwerkdimension, -struktur und -form, betrifft, wobei folgende Einwände vorgebracht bzw. folgende Mängel und Unzulänglichkeiten aufgewiesen worden sind:
1. Die von vornherein festgelegte Wahl der Anzahl der Netzwerkeinheiten, d.h. der Netzwerkgröße (oder -dimension), die die erreichbare Abbildungsgenauigkeit der Standard SOM bestimmt, kann dazu führen, daß „man im ungünstigsten Fall eine ganze Reihe von Versuchen benötigt, um die richtige Netzwerkgröße herauszufinden", sei es für den Fall, daß man zu wenige Neuronen verwendet hat, weshalb, bei nicht ausreichender Abbildungsgenauigkeit für die beabsichtigte Anwendung, der gesamte Simulationsprozeß mit einer höheren Anzahl von Neuronen wiederholt werden müßte, oder, sei es für den Fall, daß man zu viele Neuronen verwendet hat, weshalb, um einen erwünschten entsprechend geringeren Speicherplatz- und Rechenzeitbedarf zu erzielen, der gesamte Simulationsprozeß mit einer niedrigeren Anzahl von Neuronen wiederholt werden müßte.[170]
2. Auch die von vornherein festgelegte Wahl der Netzwerkstruktur und -form kann die Leistung der Standard SOM, vor allem ihre grundlegenden Eigenschaften der Topologie- und Wahrscheinlichkeits(-dichte-)erhaltung, bei bestimmten Anwendungen stark beeinflussen.[171]
Diese beiden miteinander zusammenhängenden Grundnachteile der Standard SOM kann man m.E. als h.M. in der Literatur ansehen, weshalb hierfür einige Belege angeführt werden sollen:
„A drawback of the model (= Standard SOM (A.d.V.)) is that the topology has to be fixed in advance although an appropriate choice of the topology can in general be made only by taking into account unavailable statistical properties of the given data."[172]
„(...) a neighborhood preserving mapping from input to output space is established, provided the map output space matches the topology of the data manifold in the input space. If this is not the case (...), the SOM algorithm cannot possibly achieve a neighborhood preserving projection (...). As the effective dimensionality of a data manifold in the input space is most often (a priori) unknown, straightforward application of the SOM with fixed output space topology does not guarantee an optimal neighborhood preservation."[173]
„One of the drawbacks of the SOM is that the user must select the map size in advance. This may lead to many experiments with different sized maps, trying to obtain the optimal result. This is very time consuming."[174][175]
„The self organising map is normally represented as a two dimensional grid of nodes. The size of the grid and as such the number of nodes has to be pre-determined. (...)
Thus with the original Kohonen map, we cannot ever be confident that a particular set of clusters is the most appropriate structure. A cluster could be

- 44 -

made up of some sub clusters which are not apparent due to the size limitation of the network."[176]

„The traditional SOM does not provide a measure for identifying the size of a
feature map with it's level of spread. Therefore the data analyst using the SOM
can only refer to the length and width of the grid to relate to map size. We
show that the shape or size of the SOM cannot be meaningfully related to the
spread of the data without accurate knowledge of the distribution of the
data set."[177]

„The self-organizing feature map's (...) primary use as a computational tool is
in forming a mapping from a high-dimensional input space to two dimensions.
(...) However, accurately representing high-dimensional structure on a continuous, fully connected $n \times m$ grid is problematic. Discontinuities in the input
space may appear bridged in the map. The map may have connections that
span the disjoint clusters, or it may have nodes situated within the discontinuity
where the input probability is 0 (...). In other words, the final feature map
sometimes misrepresents the topology of the input data."[178]

„(...) hierarchical relations between the input data are not mirrored in a
straight-forward manner. Such relations are rather shown in the same representation space and are thus hard to identify. Hierarchical relations, however,
may be observed in a wide spectrum of application domains, thus their proper identification remains a highly important data mining task that cannot be
addressed conveniently within the framework of the SOM."[179]

3. Desweiteren benötigt der Standard SOM-Algorithmus, vor allem für die Suche nach dem „Gewinner"-Neuron bei einer hohen Anzahl von Neuronen,
   eine zu hohe Rechenzeit:

„The computing time of the above algorithm (= original SOM algorithm (A.d.
V.)) is dominated by the search of the best matching unit (BMU). The original
algorithm (...) uses full search where all the neurons are visited to find the BMU.
(...)
The computing time of the original SOM increases linearly when the number
of reference vectors (neurons) is increased. (...)
Thus SOM is computationally costly in high input dimensions or when the number of neurons is large."[180]

„A problem with large SOMs is that when the map size is increased, the time it
takes to do any operations on the map increases linearly. Training and using
these large maps may again be quite slow."[181]

„A central parameter affecting the resolution of the SOM is the area of its
map size. With a linearly increasing map area, the number of nodes in a SOM
increase quadratically. Therefore, the training of large maps can be computationally quite expensive."[182]

4. Auch die hierarchischen Strukturen der Eingangsdaten kann die Standard
   SOM nur ungenügend modellieren:

„(...) the basic SOM lacks the ability to extract the hierarchical structure of the
data."[183]

5. Ferner kann auch die diskrete Natur der Standard SOM eine Unzulänglich-
   keit darstellen:

„However, the discrete nature of the standard SOM can be a limitation when the construction of smooth, higher-dimensional map manifolds is desired. Since the number of nodes grows exponentially with the number of map dimensions, manageably sized lattices with, say, more than three dimensions (...) admit only very few nodes along each axis direction and can, therefore, be not sufficiently smooth for many purposes where continuity is very important, as e.g. in (...) robotics."[184]

6. Abschließend wird noch auf den sgn.„border" oder „boundary effect" (dt. „Grenzeffekt") von Knoten in den Netzwerkecken oder in der Nähe davon hingewiesen, wonach die Euklidische Distanz zwischen den Gewichtsvektoren der „Grenz-" oder „Randknoten" (engl.„border nodes") und den Gewichtsvektoren der nächst „inneren Knoten" (engl.„inner nodes") gewöhnlich geringer ist als die Euklidische Distanz zwischen zwei inneren Knoten im Zentrum des Netzwerks, was nahe der Randknoten Abbildungsverzerrungen erzeugt:

„One of the problems that appears in these networks is due to the asymmetry of the architecture. The nodes located at the extreme of the network have fewer neighborhoods than the internal nodes. This fact (...) produces a distortion near the border nodes. It causes an asymmetry in the correct weight vectors of the border nodes, which are more often pulled towards the inner nodes (...)."[185] [186]

7.2 KRITIK AN DEN GROWING SOM VARIANTS

7.20 Eine generelle Kritik der „Growing SOM Variants" lautet wie folgt: „It can be stated, however, that the main focus of each of these adaptive variants of the Self-Organizing Map lies with an equal distribution of the input patterns across the map by adding new units in the neighborhood of units that represent an unproportionally high number of input data. They thus do not primarily reflect the concept of representation at a certain level of detail, which is expressed in terms of the overall quantization error rather than in the number of input data mapped onto specific areas. Moreover, neither of these adaptive models takes the inherently hierarchical structure of data into account."[187]

„These methods employ heuristics to ensure that nodes are added only where the network needs them to represent the input space, and that nodes are deleted only when they do not represent any part of the input space. Most of the resulting networks, however, have arbitrary dimensionality and connectivity. There is no guarantee the final network structure can be easily visualized in two dimensions."[188]

„One of the main drawbacks of these methods is that it is difficult to visualise high dimensional data and levels of clustering. Although the intra-cluster similarities can be repesented it is difficult to measure inter-cluster similarities and memberships of documents belonging to different classes."[189] „Generally, these methods may continue growing, resulting in a very large structure and long training times. It is difficult to navigate the map. To solve these issues the hierarchical models have been combined with the growing variants."[190]

„When the grid size becomes very large, finding the best matching unit takes longer and longer. Larger maps require some sort of additional data structures that make the search faster."[191]

„(...) the greater part of single-stage networks based on Kohonen's network have a great difficulty in solving the classification problem of large-set patterns due to their inherent limitations in structural aspect of the network. Furthermore, as the network size becomes larger, the computational complexity of the learning process quickly reaches unmanageable proportions."[192]

7.21 Die „Growing Grid (GG)"- Methode B. FRITZKE's besitzt gegenüber der Standard SOM gewisse Vorzüge: „Self-organizing models with a pre-defined structure, in particular the self-organizing feature map of Kohonen, may have difficulties to properly represent data manifolds with a topology not matching the network topology." (...)[193]

The Growing Grid network „automatically chooses a height/weight ratio suitable for the data distribution at hand. Locally accumulated statistical values are used to decide where to insert new units. (...) The new units are orderly inserted by interpolating their refence vectors from their neighbors. This makes topological defect – known from other models – very rare" and „guarantees local order in the map and in nearly all cases also leads to global ordering. All parameters in the model are constant eliminating the need to decide in advance on the total number of adaptation steps."[194]

Demgegenüber wenden R.T. FREEMAN / H. YIN[195] ein, daß die GG-Methode mit folgendem Nachteil behaftet sei: „The disadvantage is that the map may become very large after a few insertions (since no heuristic methods are used for node deletion) and some resources may be underused." Dem kann m.E. entgegengehalten werden, daß B. FRITZKE für diesen Fall ausdrücklich ein sgn. „stopping criteria" eingeführt hat: „To prevent the network from growing indefinitely a stopping criterion has to be defined."[196]

Desweiteren betont B. FRITZKE die Vorteile einer rechtwinkligen Netzform der GG-Methode im Vergleich zu anderen dynamischen Modellen: „The network can be displayed trivially by drawing a grid and the implementation does not require the handling of graphs or other sophisticated data structures. An array suffices to represent the network."[197]

7.22 Das „Growing Self-Organizing Map (GSOM)"- Modell von H.-U. BAUER und Th. VILLMANN zeichnet sich durch den Vorteil eines verbesserten Grads an Topologie- und Nachbarschaftserhaltung aus: „The aim of the GSOM is to generate lattice structures with an improved degree of topology preservation remaining the hupercube structure. During the learning procedure not only the pointers are distributed in the data space. In addition the dimension of A is adapted and also the lenght ratios between the lattice directions, i.e. a structure adaptation takes place."[198]

„After having seen why neighborhood preservation in neural maps can be advantageous, we now turn to a discussion of the different ways to ensure it. We pointed out (...), that two components of the self-organization process have to match: the output space topology has to roughly match that of the data distribution, and the map self-organization process itself has to be correctly parametrized to avoid traps. In the present paper we are concerned with the former problem, and presented the GSOM-algorithm, which adapts the output space topology to the input data, but in a constrained way. The output space is forced to maintain the shape of a generalized hypercube. This is in contrast to other approaches to this problem (...), which allowed less constrained or even completely unconstrained output space connectivities. Obviously, with less or no constraints these can possibly achieve an even better match than a GSOM. However, this comes at the expense of a more complicated connectivity structure."[199]

Demgegenüber werden in der Literatur folgende Nachteile geltend gemacht: „In contrast to the growing grid method the insertion of a new row or column is always done in the center of the existing structure no matter which units have received most input signals in the past. Perhaps because of this strategy they have to use a complicated saw-tooth-shaped decay for the neighborhood range and have to fix the final network size and the total number of adaptation steps in advance."[200]

„In contrast to the IGG algorithm, both the overall dimensionality of the grid and its extensions along the different directions are the subject of the adaptation. The criterion for growing the network is based on the fluctuations in different directions within the masked Voronoi cells of the output nodes. The computation need for this growing process is very expensive."[201]

7.23 Die Kritik am „Growing Cell Structures (GCS)"- Algorithmus B. FRITZKE's in der Literatur lautet wie folgt: This algorithm „yield an output space connectivity which is not easy to formalize as a simple structure, like e.g. as a hypercube (with varying dimensions along the different directions). Instead, it has to be described as a symmetric graph of possibly very complicated structure."[202]

„In the case of 2-dimensional input, it is easy to verify that the network accurately represents the input by plotting the weight vectors in 2-D. When the input is high-dimensional, however, such an arbitrary structure may not have a simple low-dimensional description (that is, it cannot easily be drawn in 2 dimensions). Fritzke (...) presents a drawing method based on a physical force analogy that works reasonably well when the input space is low-dimensional (e.g., 3-D), but is not guaranteed to produce a planar drawing. Also, the arbitrary connectivity makes topological neighborhoods ambiguous beyond directly connected nodes. Any node may be connected to any number of neighbors, so a neighborhood of a given radius in the structure (i.e., the number of connections outward in any direction) has little topological meaning. Thus, extracting the overall topological relationships of the input space from this structure may not be easy. The algorithm does explcitly represent clustering of the input data by removing connections between the clusters in the structure. However, the topology within clusters and across continuous data sets may be difficult to determine."[203]

„This model, however, requires much more learning parameters, related to network structure adaptation, to de adjusted in advance. Moreover, it is much more susceptible to minor variations in these parameters than the self-organizing map."[204]

„However the GCS was having difficulty to represent the input topology (...) by broken links or cross links in the output topological structure."[205]

„However, extreme plasticity can have unfortunate side-effects since useful accumulated learning experience can be lost. For instance, the deletion of a

node can be followed by massive purges in the GCS network, partly because the learning algorithm attempts to maintain a network that can be viewed as a set of hyper-tetrahedra (triangles, for 2D topology).
A little more stability would be useful: this is accomplished using the hierarchical GCS algorithm (...)."[206]
„(...) the major drawback of Cell Structures used in the context of life-long learning is their permanent increase in the number of nodes and in the drift of the centers to capture the input probability density in the unsupervised adaptation case and to reflect the error probability density in the supervised adaptation case (...). Tresholds such as a maximal number of nodes predetermined by the user as well as insertion criterion dependent on the overall error or on a quantization error are not appropriate, simply because appropriate figures for these criteria cannot be known in advance. Thus, the Cell Structures are only capable to follow an input probability density by using the utility-based removal (High plasticity) or to approximate a decision boundary by freezing the number of nodes and allowing only minor changes in the adaptation of the weights (High stability).
The catch is that these networks suffer even more from a catastrophic allocation of new nodes (...), because they permanently insert new nodes at locations with high errors."[207]
Demgegenüber besitzt das GCS-Modell im Vergleich zur Basic SOM gewisse Vorzüge, die aus ihren oben erwähnten Nachteilen entspringen: The GCS model „has the following advantages over existing models: First, the network structure is determined automatically from the input data. Second, the network size has not to be predefined. Instead, the growth process can be continued until a performance criterion is met. Third, all parameters of the model are constant. It is, therefore, not necessary to define a decay schedule as in other models. Fourth, the insertion of new units can be influenced such that the generated network estimates the probability density of the input signals, minimizes the quantization error or pursues still other goals. Fifth, since the final structure depends on the input data it can be used for data visualization and for clustering. In contrast, most other models have a fixed structure which does not provide any information of that kind."[208]
Außerdem betont B. FRITZKE, daß die Wahl der Hypertetraeder als adäquate Elemente einer variablen Netzwerkstruktur, die „sich besonders gut zu größeren Verbänden kombinieren lassen", den Vorzug genießt, „eine exakte Nachbildung von nahezu beliebig geformten n-dimensionalen Strukturen" zu ermöglichen.[209]
Abschließend wird ein Fazit von A. ZELL zitiert, das für alle „Growing Grid"- Varianten gilt: Die KOHONEN-Karten, die „die Form des Netzes der Wahrscheinlichkeitsdichtefunktion dynamisch anpassen, indem neue Neuronen gebildet und mit ihren Nachbarn verbunden werden, (...) haben den Vorteil, daß sie nicht-konvexe und sogar nicht-zusammenhängende Gebiete mit hoher Wahrscheinlichkeitsdichte besser modellieren können. Diese Verfahren (u.a. auch das GCS-Verfahren (A.d.V.)) erkaufen ihre zusätzliche Flexibilität aber mit dem Nachteil, daß die Erhaltung der Topologie und die Entfernungsbestimmung der Neuronen schwieriger ist."[210]

7.3 KRITIK AN DEN MULTILEVEL SOM VARIANTS

7.30 Die generelle Kritik an den „Multilevel SOM Variants" wird in der Literatur wie folgt vorgebracht: „However the user is required to predefine the granularity of the individual SOMs as well as the overall depth of the structure."[211] „Generally, in the hierarchical approaches the size of the maps and depth of the hierarchy are fixed. These limitations can be overcome through the use of growing SOM-variants, where the sizes of the maps are adjusted dynamically during training."[212]

„(...) the unbalance of computational load is occured in most multistage networks. In other words, the resultant network tends to be taken the form of the skewed-tree structure. It may be attributed to the following two facts: 1) weight adjustment of only a single winner node at each level from the root to the leaf and 2) undesirable adaptation of network structure."[213]

7.31 Der Vorteil des sgn.„Hierarchical Self-Organizing Map (HSOM)"- Modells von J. LAMPINEN und E. OJA, das adaptive Distanzmaß, ist bereits in Kpt. 3.11 erwähnt worden, weshalb hier ergänzende Bemerkungen angeführt werden sollen: The HSOM is suitable for clustering, because „it will produce 'natural' clusters whos form is dynamically matched to the probability density structure of the input samples. If there are low dimensional structures in the data they will form long elongated clusters, while uniform data is mapped to circular clusters." (...)

The HSOM clustering „corresponds roughly to classical clustering methods when the distance of a point from the cluster is defined as weighted distance from all the points in the cluster, but with HSOFM (=HSOM (A.d.V.)) the clustering requires only two nearest neighbor searches instead of computing all the distances and the extent of weighting is adapted automatically to the data distribution (...).

In addition, the system minimizes the total quantization error introduced by both the layers (...). Among clustering methods this is a rather unique balance between preserving maximal information and collapsing the data to natural clusters."[214]

7.32 Wie bereits erwähnt, führt die hierarchische Kooperation zwischen den Subnetzen zu einer Beschleunigung des Lernprozesses und „gewährleistet die erwünschte 'glatte' (...) Bewegung des Arms" im sgn.„Hierarchical Neural Network" von Th.M. MARTINETZ und Kl.J. SCHULTEN: „Although the number of neurons for learning the control of the orientation of the gripper in addition to arm positioning is 25 times as high as the number of neurons for arm positioning alone (...), the total number of required trial movements does not increas when the griper capability is added to the arm."[215]

7.33 In bezug auf ihren sgn.„Tree-Structured Self-Organizing Map (TS-SOM)"- Algorithmus werden von E. OJA und P. KOIKKALAINEN folgende Vorteile angeführt: „One advantage of the TS-SOM when compared to other tree structured quantization algorithms is that it introduces tolerance to upper level errors. This is done by making corrections at every tree level by using a lateral search (...). Since each tree level is a SOM network, we can use the lateral connections to see if the neighboring neurons could be better choices for the

BMU. Now the search sets from father nodes to son nodes are overlapping, the discriminant surfaces are closer to the optimal shape, and the performance is better."[216]

„TS-SOM utilizes tree search to reduce the training time complexity of the original SOM algorithm from $O(N)$ to $O(\log_p N)$, where N is the number of neurons and p is the number of sons per each tree node. (...), in some cases tree search can be improved with a lookup search to almost $O(1)$ time complexity, thus resulting that the training time is almost independent of the number of neurons."[217]

„Yet another benefit of the tree structure is that it can be used as a constructive estimator of the training set."[218]

7.34 Das sgn.„Evolving Tree"- Modell nach J. PAKKANEN, J. IIVARINEN und E. OJA zeichnet sich anhand folgender Vorzüge aus: „An ideal system could combine grid growing and hierarchical search. (...) We propose here a new variant (...) which tries to combine both of these advantages. The nodes are arranged in a tree topology that is allowed to grow when any given branch receives a lot of hits from the training vectors. The search for the best matching unit and its neighbors is conducted along the tree and its therefore very efficient."[219]

„The Evolving Tree can automatically grow new nodes, so there is no need to decide the amount of nodes in advance. The system also has a hierarchical seek structure so it can handle more nodes than would be feasible with regular SOM."[220]

„Contrary to the Tree-Structured SOM of Koikkalainen and Oja (...), which also has a hierarchical structure, the Evolving Tree does not form regular SOM layers, but each branch is free to evolve independently. This flexibility allows the Evolving Tree to adapt to data more efficiently, leading to better performance."[221]

7.4 KRITIK AN DEN GROWING HIERARCHICAL SOM VARIANTS

7.41 In der Literatur werden folgende Vorteile des „Growing Hierarchical Self-Organizing Map (GHSOM)"- Modells von D. MERKL, M.DITTENBACH, A. RAUBER et. alt. angeführt: The GHSOM addresses the problem by hierarchical SOMs in predefining the granularity of the individual SOMs as well as the overall depth of the structure „through a flexible structure which grows to fit the data. A quality measure based on the variance of the data together with threshold parameters are used to decide which granularity is appropriate for a specific SOM, and which areas of the SOM are promising candidates for further hierarchical expansion."[222] (...)

The GSOM „enhances the capabilities of the basic SOM in two ways. The first is to use an incrementally growing version of the SOM, which does not require the user to directly specify the size of the map before hand, the second enhancement is the ability to adapt to hierarchical structures in the data. Both issues have been addressed separately by means of adaptive architectures, e.g. the Growing Grid (...), or the Growing SOM (...), or hierarchies of independent SOMs, e.g., the Hierarchical Feature Map (...) or the Tree Structured SOM

(...).“[223]

D. MERKL, M. DITTENBACH, A. RAUBER et. alt. beschreiben die Vorzüge ihres Modells wie folgt: „The major feature of this model are its hierarchical architecture, where the depth of the hierarchy is determined during an unsupervised training process. Each layer in the hierarchy consists of a number of independent self-organizing maps which determine their size and arrangement of units also during the unsupervised training process. Thus, this model is especially well suited for applications which require hierarchical clustering of the input data.“[224]

Demgegenüber wird folgender Nachteil vorgebracht: „This method is autonomous and efficient in generating a hierarchy of maps, but is sensitive to parameters such as maximum growth and depth.“[225]

7.42 Der Vorteil des „Hierarchical Growing Cell Structures (TreeGCS)“- Modells besteht nach V.J. HODGE und J. AUSTIN in folgendem: „Our TreeGCS algorithm adaptively determines the depth of the cluster hierarchy; there is no requirement to prespecify network dimensions as with SOM-based algorithms“[226], wohingegen folgende Nachteile zu beachten sind: „The method is generally computationally intensive (in the order of $O(n^3)$) (...) and in a dendrogram representation most of the topological relations obtained by the GCS can be lost.“[226]

7.5 KRITIK AN DER ASSOM NACH T. KOHONEN ET. ALT.

7.51 Der Vorteil der sgn.„Adaptive Subspace Self-Organizing Map (ASSOM)“ von T. KOHONEN et. alt. besteht in der Fähigkeit zur Gewinnung von unveränderlichen Eigenschaften, was in einer Vielzahl von Experimenten bewiesen worden ist[227]: „Each processing module in the network can be made to become invariant to one transformation type and decode a certain range of features invariantly of this transformation. Different competing modules specialize in representing different kinds of invariant features. The network can thus function as a learning preprocessing stage for invariant-feature extraction.“ (...)

„An intriguing possibility that the neurons in the ASSOM architecture might have biological counterparts ensues from the forms and operation of the filters in the input and output layers. The receptive fields of the simple cells in the mammalian primary visual cortex have been hypothesized to be describable by Gabor-type functions (...), and the ASSOM process also produces Gabor-type filters in the first-layer neurons. The output-layer neurons respond invariantly to moving and transforming targets and in this sense resemble the complex cells.“[228]

Der ASSOM-Algorithmus von T. KOHONEN et. alt. wird aber wie folgt kritisiert: „ASSOM is able to extract the subspaces closest to the given sample data points, and to accurately classify data based on the extracted subspaces. ASSOM, however, requires that all vectors have zero mean; that is, the subspaces must intersect the origin of the feature space. Although this may be a valid assumption for some data, such as those found in spectra, stationary acoustic signals, etc., it is not for many others, an important example being images and videos. As shown in Kohonen's experiments, ASSOM does indeed succeed in capturing the linear subspaces inherent in small transformations. However, it may fail in such applications as image compression and classification. This is analogous to using the multi-layer feedforward backpropagation network without the bias term to the input vector. All hyper-planes in the weight space thus formed will necessarily be constrained to intersect with the origin 0. This seriously limits the general applicability and the accuracy of the network."[229]

7.6 KRITIK AN DEN ALTERNATIVE SOM VARIANTS

7.61 Das sgn.„Hyperbolic Self-Organizing Map (HSOM)"- Modell von H. RITTER / J. ONTRUP besitzt folgende Vorteile: „(...) besides the more obvious uses of spherical SOMs the newly proposed hyperbolic SOMs are characterized by very interesting scaling properties of their lattice neighborhood that makes them promising candidates to better capture the structure of very high-dimensional or hierarchical data. We have shown how regular tesselations of the hyperbolic plane H2 can be used to construct a SOM that projects onto discretized H2 and we have presented initial simulation results demonstrating that this 'hyperbolic SOM' shares with the standard SOM the robust capability to unfold into an ordered structure. We have compared its properties with the standard SOM and found that the exponential node growth towards its periphery favors the formation of mappings that are structured differently than for the euclidean SOM. Our initial simulations indicate that the faster increasing hyperbolic neighborhood can indeed facilitate the construction of space-filling map configurations that underly the dimension reduction in SOMs and that hyperbolic SOMs can visualize hierarchical data, benefitting at the same time from techniques introduced in previous work on the exploitation of hyperbolic spaces for creating good displays of tree-like structures."[230]
Die Erweiterung zum sgn. „Hierarchically Growing Hyperbolic Self-Organizing Map (H²SOM)" besitzt darüber hinaus noch folgende Vorzüge: „(...) the H²SOM manages to combine (i) a growing scheme allowing for an incremental training of an adaptive lattice structure to achieve a prescribed quantization error, (ii) a hierarchical data organization both yielding an excellent scaling behaviour and the possibility to explore the underlaying structures in data and (iii) last but not least a continuous, map-based browsing offering a natural 'focus & context' behaviour."[231]
7.62 Die Vorzüge des sgn.„Parametrized Self-Organizing Map (PSOM)"- Modells werden von H. RITTER und J. WALTER et. alt. in Kürze wie folgt beschrieben: „The PSOM algorithm can be characterized by learning from very few examples and dynamical assignment of input and output space (associative completion). Its strength is to pick up the essential curvature information of the topologically ordered training data set by constructing a smooth manifold."[232]
Etwas ausführlicher wird dies von H. RITTER ausgeführt: „The discrete representation that underlies the standard SOM algorithm poses a problem for applications where higher dimensional map manifolds together with continuity of the mapping are required. The proposed 'parametrized self-organizing map' may

offer a way to overcome this difficulty. It offers two interesting benefits:
First, it requires only a very small set of topologically ordered reference vectors, from which it constructs a map manifold in parametric form that is a good approximation to the manifold that would be obtained with the standard SOM, provided a sufficiently huge number of reference vectors could be used in that case. This can be viewed as a form of learning from very few examples: if for a small number of data samples their topological ordering is known, the full PSOM can be constructed.
Second, the resulting mapping offers the flexibility to declare any subset of variables of the embedding space that is sufficient to uniquely specify a point on the map manifold as the independent 'input' variable set, from which the values of the remaining variables can be constructed via equations 3 and 1. This can be viewed as a kind of nonlinear, 'associative' completion of a partial variable set and distinguishes a PSOM from other, 'feedforward-type'-approaches (...). Instead, the map manifold of the PSOM plays the role of a smooth attractor manifold and a dynamics for the pattern completion is given by the gradient rule equation 3. This strongly resembles the situation in associative memory networks. However, there is an important difference: most associative memory networks are intrinsically based on a discrete set of point attractors and do not allow the specification of attractors that are arbitrary smooth manifolds, as they commonly occur in robotics or in control applications."[233]
Diese Vorzüge werden jedoch nach H. RITTER durch gewisse Nachteile eingeschränkt: „Of course, these benefits also come at a price, namely the increased computational costs associated with the attractor dynamics specified by equation 3. This is a common disadvantage of all recurrent networks, if compared to the simpler but less flexible feed forward nets. For large numbers of nodes, this may become a problem on a sequential computer, however, the problem is much less severe when parallel hardware is used, since the required computations are fully parallel in the number of nodes. A second point concerns the proper choice of the step size parameter $\epsilon(t)$. If the values $\gamma(t)$ are chosen too large, the dynamics may diverge, if they are too small, unnecessarily many steps are consumed."[234]
Kritisiert wird in der Literatur das „Parametrized Self-Organizing Map (PSOM)"-Modell H. RITTER's und J. WALTER's et. alt. wie folgt: „Most often, a neural map projecting data of technical origin is embedded in a larger system which is to achieve some task. Then, subsequent operations have to be performed on the projected data. Depending on the task, a general graph structure of the output space can prohibit such further processing. (...) Here , it is essential to have not only neighborhood preservation per se, but neighborhood preservation in anorderly arrangement of neurons in the output space. (...) In the PSOM-framework, the map manifold is expanded in a small set of 'basis manifolds', with the expansion coefficients being determined at a small number of reference points. The mapping values at these reference points can be obtained using the regular SOFM-algorithm. For the expansion to work, the reference points have to span the input space in aneighborhood preserving way, and the same time have to be arranged on a (generalized hypercubical lat-

tice).
Even though (...) the embedding of the neural map in a larger system ((...) the PSOM (...)) puts constraints on the possible structure of the output space, the problem of output space adaptation to the a priori unknown structure underlying the input data remains. To get around this problem, a method is needed which can adapt output space topologies in an unsupervised way, but at the same time obeys constraints on the possible connectivity."[235] [236]

7.7 EVALUATION DER SOM VARIANTS

Zusammenfassend kann gesagt werden, daß die Growing Hierarchical SOM Variants gegenüber den Growing SOM Variants und den Multilevel SOM Variants grundsätzlich vorzuziehen sind, da sie die Vorzüge beider Variantentypen in sich vereinen, d.h. sowohl durch das Einfügen und Entfernen von Neuronen einen hohen Grad an Adaptivität aufweisen als auch die variable hierarchische Struktur der Daten angemessen wiederzugeben in der Lage sind, wie z.B. das Growing Hierarchical Self-Organizing Map - Modell von D. MERKL, M. DITTENBACH und A. RAUBER et. alt. Diese hohe Leistungsfähigkeit wird m.E. nur noch von den Tree-Structured SOM Varianten übertroffen, die ebenfalls die „Growing Grid"- Komponente mit einer (Baum-)Hierarchiestruktur koppeln und zudem noch den entscheidenden Vorzug einer schnelleren Suche nach dem Gewinnerneuron aufweisen, da bei zumeist sehr hochdimensionalen Datenstrukturen und bei komplexeren Netzwerkstrukturen, d.h. bei einer größeren Anzahl von Neuronen(-ebenen), diese aufwendige Suche zu unerwünscht hohen Rechenzeiten führen würde. M.E. besitzt daher vor allem das Evolving Tree - Modell nach J. PAKKANEN und E. OJA eine überzeugende Attraktivität auch in bezug auf seinen vergleichsweise geringen Programmier- und Implementationsaufwand bei gleichzeitiger sehr hoher Leistungsfähigkeit, weshalb es einen hohen Grad an Effizienz und – gegenüber dem Tree-Structured Self-Organizing Map - Modell von E. OJA, P. KOIKKALAINEN, J.T. LAAKSONEN und J.M. KOSKELA et. alt. – auch eine erhöhte Flexibilität in den Zweigen erreicht.
 Was die Netzwerkstruktur und -form betrifft, so kann man m.E. von folgendem allgemeinen Leitsatz ausgehen, daß nämlich diese soweit wie möglich an die jeweilige, sofern bekannte Datenstruktur anzupassen ist, d.h. z.B., daß bei einer zirkulären Datenstruktur auch eine zirkuläre Netzwerkform am angemessensten wäre. Da aber die Datenstruktur oft nicht bekannt sein dürfte, stellt eine maximal adaptive Netzform, wie z.B. das Growing Cell Structure-Modell nach B. FRITZKE m.E. eine optimale Lösung dar, jedoch immer unter der Berücksichtigung einer damit einhergehenden ebenso möglichst optimalen Topologie- und Nachbarschaftserhaltung. Sollen überdies auch hierarchische Strukturen berücksichtigt werden, stellt das Hierarchical Growing Cell Structures - Modell nach V.J. HODGE und J. AUSTIN die beste Lösung dar.
 Abschließend sei darauf hingewiesen, daß die Standard SOM[237] und deren Varianten[238] auch im Bereich der Künstlichen Intelligenz und der Robotik Anwendung finden.

1 KOHONEN 2001: 350-52
2 FREEMAN / YIN 2004: 1258-60
3 KASKI 1997: 27-28
4 SI / LIN / VUONG 2000 : 617-18
5 SUGANTHAN 1999: 193
6 VESANTO 2000: 18-20
7 KOHONEN 2001: 105
8 KOHONEN 2001: 106
9 ZELL 1997: 186
10 KOHONEN 2001: 110
11 KOHONEN 1995.1: 112 und 2001: 159-60 sowie KOHONEN / KANGAS / LAAKSONEN 1992: Kpt.3
12 KOHONEN 2001: 200
13 KOHONEN 2001: 350
14 Sehr ausführlich in KOHONEN 2001: 105-76, v.a. 106-12 und in KOHONEN 1988: 119-57, v.a. 130-33, kurz in KOHONEN 2002: 1-3 und 1998: 2-3 und KOHONEN / KANGAS / LAAKSONEN 1990, erstmalig in KOHONEN 1982.1: 60-63, KOHONEN 1982.3 und KOHONEN 1982.2. Weitere gute Einführungen sind zu finden in RITTER / MARTINETZ / SCHULTEN 1990: 67-84, v.a. 74-77 und ZELL 1997: 179-87, HAYKIN 1999: 443-83, ROJAS 1993: 339-59, MÜLLER / REINHARDT / STRICKLAND 1995: 167-69, 291-95, BRAUSE 1995: 140-69, KRATZER: 108-12, SCHERER 1997: 93-107, 61-65, daneben auch in FRITZKE 1992. 2: 13-19 und LAMPINEN / OJA 1992: 3-4
15 KOHONEN 2001: 110 und KOHONEN 1982.3: 118
16 KOHONEN 2001: 111 und KOHONEN 1982.3: 119
17 KOHONEN 2002: 2-3
18 FRITZKE 1992.2: 14-16
19 Eine grundlegende Behandlung der Gewinner- und Nachbarschaftsfunktion findet sich in KOHONEN 2001: 110-12. Den komprimierten Algorithmus findet man am anschaulichsten in RITTER / MARTINETZ / SCHULTEN 1990: 74, ROJAS 1993: 344, SCHERER 1997: 101, BRAUN / FEULNER / MALAKA 1996: 63 und FRITZKE 1992.2: 19, im Detail in Van HULLE 2000: 19. Eine physiologische Interpretation des SOM-Algorithmus, insbesondere der „Winner Take All (WTA) function" und der „neighborhood function", bietet KOHONEN 1993: 896-904 und KOHONEN 2001: 177-89.
20 GROSSBERG 1976
21 von der MALSBURG 1973 und von der MALSBURG / WILLSHAW 1976, einführend Van HULLE 2000: 13-15. Für eine Herleitung des KOHONEN-Modells aus dem WILLSHAW- und von der MALSBURG-Modell siehe DERSCH 1995: 23-42.
22 KOHONEN 2001: 172-75, 193, 199-200 und KOHONEN 2002: 8
23 KOHONEN 2001: 192, 197-98
24 KOHONEN 2001: 200 (s. Text S. 2)
25 KOHONEN 2001: 193
26 KOHONEN 2001: 216-43
27 KOHONEN 2002: 7-9
28 KOHONEN 2002: 9-10, ausführlicher KOHONEN 2001: 263-310
29 KOHONEN 1988: 241-68
30 KOHONEN 2001: 347-72, v.a. bzgl. alternativer Architekturtypen KOHONEN 2001: 350-52
31 FRITZKE 1996: 61
32 FREEMAN / YIN 2004: 1259
33 erstmalig präsentiert in FRITZKE 1995.1
34 FRITZKE 1996: 64
35 FRITZKE 1995.1: 9
36 FRITZKE 1995.1: 9-10
37 FRITZKE 1995.1: 10
38 FRITZKE 1995.1: 10-11
39 FRITZKE 1995.1:11
40 zum ersten Mal und am ausführlichsten veröffentlicht in BAUER / VILLMANN 1995.1, daneben in BAUER / VILLMANN 1995.2, 1997 und, Anwendungen betreffend BAUER / VILLMANN 1998 sowie einführend VILLMANN 1999 und VILLMANN / MERÉNYI 2002
41 BAUER / VILLMANN 1997: 287, VILLMANN 1999: 285 und VILLMANN / MERÉNYI 2002: 126
42 VILLMANN 1999: 286; siehe auch VILLMANN / MERÉNYI 2002 : 126 und ausführlich BAUER / VILLMANN 1997.1: 223
43 BAUER / VILLMANN 1995.1: 223-24
44 VILLMANN 1999: 286-87; siehe auch VILLMANN / MERÉNYI 2002 : 126 und ausführlich BAUER / VILLMANN 1995.1: 223-27, v.a. 224 m. Abb. 3.2

45 zuerst veröffentlicht in MIIKKULAINEN / BLACKMORE 1993 und danach in MIIKKULAINEN / BLACK-MORE 1995

46 MIIKKULAINEN / BLACKMORE 1993: 453 und 1995: 57-58. Was den detaillierten IGG-Algorithmus betrifft, wird auf die Textstellen in MIIKKULAINEN / BLACKMORE 1993: 451-53, v.a. 451 mit Abb. 2 und 1995: 56-58 verwiesen.

47 veröffentlicht in MIIKKULAINEN / BEDNAR / KELKAR 2002: 280-84 und 2002: 351-52; grundlegend hierzu siehe z.B. MIIKKULAINEN 1992, MIIKKULAINEN / SIROSH 1992, MIIKKULAINEN 1993, MIIKKULAI-NEN / SIROSH 1994, MIIKKULAINEN / SIROSH 1993 und MIIKKULAINEN / CHOE / SIROSH 1996

48 FARKAS / LI 2002: 553-55

49 erstmalig veröffentlicht in ALAHAKOON / HALGAMUGE / SRINIVASAN 1998.1, danach in ALAHA-KOON / HALGAMUGE 1998.2, ALAHAKOON / HALGAMUGE / SRINIVASAN 1998.3, am ausführlich-sten in ALAHAKOON / HALGAMUGE / SRINIVASAN 2000, mit kurzen Einführungen in ALAHA-KOON / HALGAMUGE / HSU / SRINIVASAN 2000.1 und 2000.2 und in der neuesten Fassung in ALA-HAKOON 2004

50 Was den detaillierten IGG-Algorithmus betrifft, wird auf die Textstellen in den Artikeln von ALAHA-KOON / HALGAMUGE / SRINIVASAN 2000: 603-609 und ALAHAKOON 2004: 169-70 verwiesen.

51 HSU / HALGAMUGE 2001.1: 2-4

52 HSU / HALGAMUGE 2001.2: 1787-91

53 HSU / HALGAMUGE 2003: 261-62

54 NÜRNBERGER 2001 und NÜRNBERGER / DETYNIECKI 2002: 1913-14

55 MONNERJAHN 1996: 2-15

56 CHO 1997.1: 1348-50 und 1997.2: 48-50

57 erstmalig veröffentlicht in SEIFFERT / MICHAELIS 1996: 352-53, basierend auf der sgn.„Three Dimen-sional SOM" in SEIFFERT / MICHAELIS 1995: 311-12, und der daran anschließende sgn.„(Growing) Quasi-Four-Dimensional-Neuroncube", erstmalig publiziert in SEIFFERT / MICHAELIS / SCHÜNE-MANN 1997: 295-97, einführend SEIFFERT 1998, danach in SEIFFERT / MICHAELIS 1998.1: 78-79 und 1998.2: 44-46 und zusammenfassend SEIFFERT 2002: 95-120

58 LEE / PETERSON 1990: 1459-64

59 RODRIGUES / ALMEIDA 1990: 814-15

60 JOKUSCH 1990: 169-72, einführend FRITZKE 1992.2: 56-58

61 FRITZKE 1992.2: 56

62 JOKUSCH 1990: 169-71, v.a. 171 m. Abb. 3

63 erstmalig präsentiert in FRITZKE 1991.1, danach am ausführlichsten beschrieben in FRITZKE 1992.2 und 1994, desweiteren in FRITZKE 1992.1 und 1993.1, einführend FRITZKE 1992.3 und in einer An-wendung zur „Vector Quantization" in FRITZKE 1993.2 und 1993.3

64 FRITZKE 1992.2: 63

65 FRITZKE 1992.2: 64

66 FRITZKE 1992.2: 64; siehe auch FRITZKE 1994: 1442 und 1996: 63

67 FRITZKE 1992.2: 67-70, v.a. 67-68; siehe auch FRITZKE 1992.1: 1052-53, FRITZKE 1991.1: 405-406 und FRITZKE 1996: 63

68 Der Algorithmus für das Verfahren der Wachsenden Zellstrukturen findet sich in FRITZKE 1992.2: 71.

69 im einzelnen siehe FRITZKE 1992.2: 74-77

70 Zum sgn.„growing and splitting elastic net" im Rahmen der Vektorquantisierung (engl.„vector quantization") siehe die fast identischen Artikel FRITZKE 1993.2 und 1993.3.

71 BRUSKE / SOMMER 1995.1 und 1995.2: 851-53, weiterentwickelt in BRUSKE / SOMMER / AHRNS 1995.3: 142-44

72 BRUSKE / SOMMER 1995.2: 850

73 CHENG / ZELL 1999: 430-36

74 CHENG / ZELL 2000: 234-36 und 2001: 91-93

75 CHENG / ZELL 2000: 234

76 DENG / WU 2001: 271-73

77 WANG / RAU / PENG 2000: 587-92

78 MERKL / KÖHLE 1996: 581-83

79 SI / LIN / VUONG 2000: 618-20

80 MIKAMI / WADA 2001: 623-24

81 SAITO / OHTA 2001: 469-70

82 VLASSIS / DIMOPOULOS / PAPAKONSTANTINOU 1997: 650-53

83 KOHONEN 2001: 350

84 KOHONEN 2001: 350-51

85 erstmals veröffentlicht in LAMPINEN 1991.1 und 1991.2, daneben in LAMPINEN 1992 und am aus-führlichsten in LAMPINEN / OJA 1992

86 LAMPINEN 1992: 1219 und LAMPINEN / OJA 1992: 261

87 LAMPINEN / OJA 1992: 268-70

88 LAMPINEN / OJA 1992: 267

89 LAMPINEN 1992: 1221

90 LAMPINEN / OJA 1992: 269 und LAMPINEN 1992: 1221

91 veröffentlicht in MARTINETZ / SCHULTEN 1990 in Verbindung mit MARTINETZ / SCHULTEN / RITTER 1989.1 und 1989.2, siehe im Detail RITTER / MARTINETZ / SCHULTEN: 175-209, vor allem 199-207

92 MARTINETZ / SCHULTEN 1990: 750-51

93 CARPINTEIRO 1996.1, CARPINTEIRO / BARROW 1996.2: 2-5, CARPINTEIRO 1997: 485-86 und CARPIN-TEIRO 2000: 280-81

94 CARPINTEIRO / BARROW 1996.2: 4

95 CARPINTEIRO / REIS / FILHO 2004

96 VERSINO / GAMBARDELLA 1995 und 1996: 222-24

97 VESANTO / ALHONIEMI / HOLLMÉN / SIMULA 1996: 775-76

98 VESANTO / ALHONIEMI / HOLLMÉN / SIMULA 1996: 775

99 ZHANG / MLYNSKI 1997: 301-12

100 HERRMANN / DER / BALZUWEIT 1996: 1390-92

101 WEIERICH / v. ROSENBERG 1994.1: 247 und 1994.2: 612-13

102 CHEN / SCHUFFELS / ORWIG 1996: 92-93

103 CHEN / ROUSSINOV 1998: 85-89

104 YE / LO 2000: 271-72

105 TAKATSUKA / JARVIS 2001: 102-13 und 1998

106 erstmals veröffentlicht unter der früheren Bezeichnung „Tree-Structured Topological Feature Map (TSTFM)" in KOIKKALAINEN / OJA 1990 i.V.m. LAMPINEN / OJA 1989, danach ausführlich in KOIKKALAINEN 1993, 1994, 1995 und 1999

107 Zur Struktur der sgn.„hyper-pyramid" siehe im einzelnen KOIKKALAINEN 1994: 212, KOIKKALAINEN 1993: 52-53 und KOIKKALAINEN 1999: 127, zu den Vorteilen des TS-SOM-Algorithmus siehe KOIKKA-LAINEN 1994: 212.

108 Eine Anwendung von TS-SOMs bildet „PisSOM", ein Bildverarbeitungssystem, in OJA / LAAKSO-NEN / KOSKELA 1999.2, 1999.3, 1999.4, 1999.5 und OJA / KOSKELA / LAAKSONEN / LAAKSO 2000.

109 Der TS-SOM-Algorithmus selbst wird beschrieben in KOIKKALAINEN / OJA 1990: 280-83, am bes-ten in KOIKKALAINEN 1994: 212-13 und 1995: 53-55.

110 KOIKKALAINEN 1994: 213

111 erstmals veröffentlicht in PAKKANEN 2003: 311-12, danach in PAKKANEN / OJA / IIVARINEN 2004: 200-203

112 PAKKANEN / OJA / IIVARINEN 2004: 200-203

113 ALAHAKOON / HALGAMUGE / HSU / SRINIVASAN 2000.1: 258-59 und 2000.2: '2-3'

114 MIIKKULAINEN 1990: 89-93

115 MIIKKULAINEN 1990: 90

116 MERKL 1997: 187-89

117 LUTTRELL 1988: 93-96, 1989.1: 405-406, 1989.2: 4-6, 1989.3 mit Einführung des sgn.„robust hidden layer principle" in LUTTRELL 1990: 229-32, und des sgn.„self-supervision principle" in LUTTRELL 1991: 2-12

118 RAHMEL 1996.1: 1404 und 1996.2: 1222-24

119 WEN / LIU / JENNINGS 1992 und WEN / PANG / JENNINGS 1993: 1469-70

120 COSTA / NETTO / NETO / BARBALHO 2001: 444 und COSTA / NETTO 2001: 21-23

121 COSTA / NETTO / NETO 2003: '2-3'

122 TRUONG / MERSEREAU 1990: 2289-91 und TRUONG 1991: 2789-91

123 DOPAZO / CARAZO 1997: 227-29

124 SONG / LEE 1998: 372-75

125 KEMKE / WICHERT 1993: 45-46

126 FREEMAN / YIN 2004: 1259-60

127 erstmalig veröffentlicht in MERKL / DITTENBACH / RAUBER 2000, danach in MERKL / DITTENBACH / RAUBER 2001.1 und 2002.2, am ausführlichsten in MERKL / RAUBER 2000, MERKL / DITTENBACH / RAUBER 2002.1 und 2002.3 und Anwendungen betreffend in MERKL / DITTENBACH / RAUBER 2001.2

128 MERKL / DITTENBACH / RAUBER 2000: 16-17 m. Abb. 1 und 2

129 Das ausführliche mathematische Modell findet sich in MERKL / RAUBER 2000: 385-88, MERKL / DITTENBACH / RAUBER 2002.1: 204-209 und MERKL / DITTENBACH / RAUBER 2002.3: 1335-39.

130 MERKL / DITTENBACH / RAUBER / HE 2003: 295-96

131 MERKL / DITTENBACH / RAUBER / HE 2003: 293

132 PAMPALK / WIDMER / CHAN 2004: 138-44

133 SUGANTHAN 1999: 193-94, siehe auch SUGANTHAN 1998: 2257-58

134 HODGE / AUSTIN 2001: 208-209 und 2002: 828-31

135 HODGE / AUSTIN 2001: 209

136 HODGE / AUSTIN 2002: 829

137 MERKL / KÖHLE 1996: 583-84

138 BURZEVSKI / MOHAN 1996: '3-6'

139 FREEMAN / YIN 2004: 1260-65

140 HUNG / LIN 1994: 628-30

141 erstmalig veröffentlicht in KOHONEN 1995.1, danach in KOHONEN 1995.2, 1995. 3, 1996.2, KO-HONEN / KASKI / LAPPALAINEN 1997, einführend KOHONEN 1996.1 und KOHONEN / KASKI / LAP-PALAINEN / SALOJÄRVI 1997, am ausführlichsten in KOHONEN 2001

142 KOHONEN 2001: 217-18

143 KOHONEN 2001: 222

144 KOHONEN 2001: 223

145 KOHONEN 2001: 225

146 KOHONEN / KASKI / LAPPALAINEN 1997: 1331-32, KOHONEN 2001: 225-26, 233-34, KOHONEN 1995.3: 21-22, KOHONEN / KASKI / LAPPALAINEN / SALOJÄRVI 1997: 193

147 Das Kernstück des ASSOM-Modells wird besonders gut beschrieben in KOHONEN 1995.2: 3-10, 1995.3: 18-22, 1996.2: 65-70 bzw. 281-86 und KOHONEN / KASKI / LAPPALAINEN 1997: 1322-32.

148 BAUER / MAYER / HERRMANN / GEISEL 1998: 962-64

149 LIU 2002: 524-27

150 ZHANG / FU / YAN / JABRI 1999

151 SPECKMANN / RADDATZ / ROSENSTIEL 1994.1: 252, 1994.2: 343 und am ausführ-lichsten 1994.3: 152-53, siehe auch SPECKMANN 1995

152 erstmals veröffentlicht in RITTER 1999

153 ONTRUP / H. RITTER 2001.1 und 2001.2

154 ONTRUP / RITTER 2005

155 RITTER 1999: 100-105

156 ITO / MIYOSHI / MASUYAMA 2000: 241

157 ANDREU / CRESPO / VALIENTE 1997: 1342-43

158 KNOPF / SANGOLE 2001: 760-62

159 KNOPF / SANGOLE 2001: 760

160 McGLINCHEY / FYFE 1997: 92-94

161 NEAGOE 1996: 677-79

162 KIANG / KULKARNI / LOUIS 2001: 95-96; siehe auch KIANG / KULKARNI / GOUL / PHILIPPAKIS / CHI / TURBAN 1997: 523

163 zum ersten Mal veröffentlicht in RITTER 1993, danach in RITTER / WALTER 1995, WALTER 1998, RIT-TER / WALTER / NÖLKER 2000, mit einer Anwendung in der „Robot Control" in RITTER 1997, weiter-entwickelt zum sgn.„Hierarchical" oder „Multiple Parametrized Self-Organizing Map" in RITTER / WALTER 1996.1, 1996.2, 1996.3

164 RITTER 1993: 569-71

165 WALTER 1998: 2055, RITTER / WALTER / NÖLKER 2000: 759

166 erstmals veröffentlicht in WEIJTERS 1995: 13-14, danach in WEIJTERS / Van den BOSCH / Van den HERIK / POSTMA 1996: 158-59, WEIJTERS / Van den BOSCH / Van den HERIK 1997.1: 28-29, 1997.2: 237-38, 1998: '1-2', WEIJTERS / Van den BOSCH 1998: 564-65

167 WEIJTERS 1995: 13

168 SU / CHANG 2001: 154-56

169 grundlegend z.B. FRITZKE 1992.2: 45-51

170 ausführlich FRITZKE 1992.2: 50

171 ausführlich FRITZKE 1992.2: 50-51

172 FRITZKE 1995.1: 9 und ebenso 1993.1: 124, 128-29

173 BAUER / VILLMANN 1998: 92; siehe auch BAUER / VILLMANN 1995.1: 218-19

174 PAKKANEN / OJA / IIVARINEN 2004: 199, siehe auch PAKKANEN 2003: 311

175 Derselbe Einwand findet sich z.B. auch in CHENG / ZELL 1999: 425, 2000: 233, 2001: 89, MERKL / DITTENBACH / RAUBER 2001.1: 140, 2002.3 : 1332, 2002.1: 200, 2002.2: 626, MERKL / DITTENBACH / RAUBER / HE 2003: 293, MERKL / RAUBER 2000: 384, ALAHAKOON / HALGAMUGE / SRINIVASAN 2000: 601-602, ALAHAKOON / HALGAMUGE / HSU / SRINIVASAN 2000.1: 257, 2000.2: '1', HSU / HAL-GAMUGE 2001.1: '1', SONG / LEE 1998: 370, CHEN / ROUSSINOV 1998: 81

176 ALAHAKOON / HALGAMUGE 1998.2: 907-908, siehe auch ALAHAKOON / HALGAMUGE / SRINIVA-SAN 2000: 602, ALAHAKOON / HALGAMUGE / HSU / SRINIVASAN 2000.2 : '1'

177 ALAHAKOON 2004: 168

178 MIIKKULAINEN / BLACKMORE 1993: 450, siehe auch 1995: 55

179 MERKL / DITTENBACH / RAUBER / HE 2003: 293, ebenso MERKL / DITTENBACH / RAUBER 2002.3: 1331, 1334, MERKL / DITTENBACH / RAUBER 2002.2: 626, 2002.1: 200, 2001.2: 201, 2001.1: 140, MERKL / RAUBER 2000: 384, PAMPALK / WIDMER / CHAN 2004: 132

180 KOIKKALAINEN 1994: 211

181 PAKKANEN / OJA / IIVARINEN 2004: 199, siehe auch PAKKANEN 2003: 311

182 ONTRUP / RITTER 2005: '1'

183 PAMPALK / WIDMER / CHAN 2004: 132

184 RITTER 1993: 569

185 ANDREU / CRESPO / VALIENTE 1997: 1341-42

186 Derselbe Einwand findet sich auch in KIANG / KULKARNI / GOUL / PHILIPPAKIS / CHI / TURBAN 1997: 521, KIANG / KULKARNI / LOUIS 2001: 93 und ITO / MIYOSHI / MASUYAMA 2000: 239, 240-41.

187 MERKL / DITTENBACH / RAUBER 2002.3 (pre-print): '4'

188 MIIKKULAINEN / BLACKMORE 1995: 55

189 FREEMAN / YIN 2004: 1259 mit Hinweis auf MERKL 1998: 74

190 FREEMAN / YIN 2004: 1259

191 PAKKANEN 2003: 311 und PAKKANEN / OJA / IIVARINEN 2004: 200

192 SONG / LEE 1998: 371

193 FRITZKE 1995.1: 11

194 FRITZKE 1995.1: 12 i.V.m. 9

195 FREEMAN / YIN 2004: 1259

196 FRITZKE 1995.1: 10

197 FRITZKE 1995.1: 9

198 VILLMANN 1999: 285

199 BAUER / VILLMANN 1995.1: 19, ebenso BAUER / VILLMANN 1998: 98-99

200 FRITZKE 1995.1: 12, ebenso 1996: 65

201 SI / LIN / VUONG 2000: 618

202 BAUER / VILLMANN 1995.1: 2-3 und VILLMANN 1999: 280

203 MIIKKULAINEN / BLACKMORE 1993: 451, ebenso ALAHAKOON / HALGAMUGE / SRINIVASAN 2000: 602 und SI / LIN / VUONG 2000: 626

204 MERKL 1997: 193

205 SI / LIN / VUONG 2000: 626

206 BURZEVSKI / MOHAN 1996: '1'

207 Hamker 2001: 553

208 FRITZKE 1994: 1471, ebenso FRITZKE 1996: 70, 1991.1: 408, 1992.1: 1054, 1993.1: 129 und CHENG / ZELL 1999: 426 und 2000: 233

209 FRITZKE 1992.2: 116

210 ZELL 1997: 186-87

211 PAMPALK / WIDMER / CHAN 2004: 132

212 FREEMAN / YIN 2004: 1259

213 SONG / LEE 1998: 371

214 LAMPINEN 1991.2: 100, 101

215 MARTINETZ / SCHULTEN 1990: 751

216 KOIKKALAINEN 1994: 212

217 KOIKKALAINEN 1995: 63, ebenso KOIKKALAINEN 1999: 126, im einzelnen hierzu KOIKKALAINEN 1994: 212 und 1993: 55-56

218 im einzelnen hierzu siehe KOIKKALAINEN 1994: 212

219 PAKKANEN / OJA / IIVARINEN 2004: 199, 200

220 PAKKANEN 2003: 315

221 PAKKANEN / OJA / IIVARINEN 2004: 210

222 PAMPALK / WIDMER / CHAN 2004: 132

223 PAMPALK / WIDMER / CHAN 2004: 135

224 MERKL / DITTENBACH / RAUBER 2000: 19, im einzelnen siehe hierzu MERKL / DITTENBACH / RAUBER 2002.3 (pre-print): '8-9', '16', was u.a. die Vorteile gegenüber dem HFM und der Basic SOM betrifft

225 FREEMAN / YIN 2004: 1260

226 HODGE / AUSTIN 2001: '4'

227 siehe im einzelnen v.a. KOHONEN 2001: 228-42

228 KOHONEN / KASKI / LAPPALAINEN 1997: 1342-43

229 LIU 2002: 522-23 unter Hinweis auf ZURADA 1992

230 RITTER 1999: 108

231 ONTRUP / RITTER 2005: '7'
232 RITTER / WALTER 1995: '10'
233 RITTER 1993: 573-74
234 RITTER 1993: 574, siehe auch RITTER / WALTER / NÖLKER 2000: 764, WALTER 1998: 2059, RITTER 1997: 683
235 BAUER / VILLMANN 1995.1: 3, ebenso VILLMANN 1999: 279-80
236 Die Vorteile der Weiterentwicklung zum sgn.„Hierarchical" oder „Multiple Parametrized Self-Organizing Map" findet man in RITTER / WALTER 1996.1: 146, 1996.2: '7-8' und 1996.3: '6-7'.
237 S. z.B. SPECKMANN 1996 Kpt. 3 und 4
238 S. z.B. MARTINETZ / SCHULTEN 1990, LUTTRELL 1988, MIIKKULAINEN 1990 und VLASSIS / DIMOPOULOS / PAPAKONSTANTINOU 1997

www.ingramcontent.com/pod-product-compliance
Lightning Source LLC
LaVergne TN
LVHW082347060326
832902LV00017B/2712